SEXTET

by Judy Jackson

Marsons London

First published in 2014 by Marsons

© Judy Jackson 2014
Printed in Great Britain

Text design by Rachel Jackson
Cover design by Rebecca Jackson

The moral right of the author has been asserted.

A CIP catalogue record for this book is available from The British Library.
ISBN 978-0-9517220-6-0

www.marsonsbooks.com

for the men in my life
Michael, Daniel, Tim, David and Adam

and the all-important women
Claudia, Emily, Karen and Melissa

part one

DEATH AND A BIRTH

Chapter 1

January 3rd 2003

A car pulls out in front of him. It's a sports saloon, edging away from the pavement in the inside lane, gliding up to the traffic lights. There is no reason to manoeuvre to the right, to be the first away when red and amber change to green.

He's in good time for his appointment. There's almost an hour before he needs to pick up the next driver—the last booking of the day. The instructor is looking forward to the lesson, with a young man who is comfortable behind the wheel. After only a month of practice he has learned to change gear without throwing the car into juddering stops and starts.

The traffic is light after the congestion along the High Road. Two lanes widen into four and the pavement on either side is almost deserted. A woman with a woollen hat wheels a baby and on the right a man is stooping by a display of vegetables. There is a single-decker approaching in the bus lane but no other traffic coming towards him.

A woman with blonde hair is standing on the pavement about fifty yards further up, on his left. Perhaps she's waiting for someone;

or looking for a taxi. The sports car has accelerated and is speeding towards the next set of lights.

He glances at the clock and breathes out, easing the seat belt. He'll park round the corner, read the sports pages and drive up to the house exactly on time. The young man is never late for the lesson, but waits at the door, with the money in his hand, in exact notes.

There's a shape moving in front of him and it's not stopping. There was nothing there a moment ago and now it's coming towards the car. His foot moves to squeeze the brakes; a thud like rubber on metal; like a toe being hit by a frozen chicken and something flying through the air. And a screeching stop and arms raised. And flashes and darkness and a still silence.

*

The ambulance crew talked and drank tea in that everyday easiness where there's nothing new to say, but endless ways of saying it. In the background was a television, flashing images to an audience that never switched off, yet rarely watched a whole programme. The room was large enough to seat eight or ten— some curled up on the faded sofas, others reading the headlines while they waited. Someone had brought in a birthday cake and was dividing it up, the knife sticking to the chocolate icing that was oozing down the sides. When the call came through, the two on duty jumped up and ran outside pulling on their jackets and blinking in the weak afternoon sun. Their shift had started before it was light and this was the fifth call of the day.

The driver shivered, testing the frost on the ground as they walked towards the ambulance. Even before both doors were shut he'd activated the computer screen to the left of the wheel. The message told them there'd been a road accident involving a young woman: "RTA female, car v. pedestrian, corner Maida Vale/ Greville Place."

A light pressure on the side of the steering wheel activated the siren. They drove out into the chill of the Edgware Road, veering right and picking up speed. Motorists froze as they heard the moan of the siren, heads turning to follow the flashing blue light. The ambulance wheeled round a traffic island, slowing, accelerating, howling through red lights. When it came to a line of stationary cars the tone changed to an insistent whine, magnified and swelling into a repeated four-note drone. Steering wheels turned to inch out of the way and allow the ambulance to cut into the inside lane. Fifty yards further on it began to weave out again to overtake on the wrong side of the road. The driver had one eye on the small screen but he had little need of the SatNav system as the route was straight ahead with no call for directional arrows to show him the way. Within minutes they were howling to a stop.

They weren't the first to arrive. A Rapid Response Unit had already been called and had been there for two minutes. Their car was positioned diagonally, blocking the oncoming traffic. The driver had already done a twenty-second survey of the scene: a car in the middle of the road; dents on the bonnet; a young woman motionless on the ground. He was bending down, waiting to see if there was any response:

"Hello, love. Can you hear me? Can you open your eyes?"

Her face didn't move. She didn't blink when they shone a light in her pupils; didn't see the crowd gathering round; couldn't hear what they were saying:

"She didn't stand a chance. She went to cross and the car hit her ... went up in the air, then she hit the ground."

Parts of a long metal frame were being unclipped from the ambulance. An oxygen mask was placed over the woman's face. A new siren announced the arrival of a police car. Two officers got out. One went over to the crashed vehicle. The motorist was sitting in his car. He lifted his head from the driving wheel and looked up. The policeman knew what he was thinking: if only he could magically erase the last ten minutes and begin his journey again. If he could do a re-run he would notice when she stepped off the kerb to walk out into the road. He would slow down and stop. Instead he was glued to the driving seat, remembering the thud when his car made contact; the blur of the shape in front of the windscreen. No-one heard as he whispered into his hands:

"I didn't see her ... she came out from nowhere. I wasn't going fast."

The second officer went over to join the ambulance team. A young woman with glasses and hair tied back was crouching down and speaking softly to the patient on the ground as she checked the woman's airways and pulse. The policeman waited, not wanting to interrupt the procedure: a plastic collar being fitted round the neck. The ambulance driver was easing the frame underneath the woman's body and fixing blocks either side of her head.

"There's bruising under her eyes and the back of her ear. Possible fractured skull. No blood from the nose or ears."

The patient was unaware of someone writing notes on the back of a tight plastic glove, or of the sound of fabric tearing as her shirt and sweater were ripped open. Had she been awake she'd have been concerned that her handbag was lying open on the road; a jumble of feminine possessions scattered on the ground. Her mobile phone was yards away; the cheery ringtone intruding into the cold silence.

A man passing by had walked on, turning his face away as he saw the impact and the body flying into the air. Others stopped and stared, watching as the patient was strapped to a trolley board. The woman wasn't moving. An oxygen mask over her face was held in place as the stretcher was raised into the back of the ambulance. The doors closed. The crowd wondered why they weren't going. The blue light was still flashing. Inside the team were taking blood pressure and measuring heart and pulse, transferring information from an overhead screen to the plastic glove and eventually to a form that had to be filled in before their arrival at the hospital.

One of the police officers rushed to the side of the ambulance, just as they were moving off.

"You'll need this. It's her stuff."

He held up the handbag, pushing in lipsticks, a mirror and an expensive spray perfume.

"There's a filofax; it'll have details of where she lives and her next of kin."

Inside the ambulance the team were putting through a call to the nearest hospital, warning of suspected head injuries. The blue light and the noise of the siren created a clear lane which immediately closed once the ambulance had gone past. It reached the ramp at South Wharf Road in the estimated six minutes. School children stood gawping as the doors were opened. The stretcher was met by a Senior House officer and a nurse. They passed through the automatic double doors, along a corridor, and turned right through another set of doors. The ambulance team transferred the patient on to one of the four beds, passing information to the waiting doctors and nurses. They were about to leave, but stayed for a moment to complete the two-page report form. Below the date January 3rd, was the name: Sophie Fielding.

If she'd been awake during the ambulance journey she would have known the names of the crew. They would have whispered "Sophie" and asked her to tell them what they needed to know. Who was her doctor? Was she on medication? Was she allergic to anything? They would have smiled and reassured her. The sight of the green uniforms and their bright young faces might have made her feel better. But Sophie was unconscious, unaware of anything that was happening.

The crew suddenly remembered they still had her handbag. On the first page of the filofax were personal details. Underneath the library membership and doctor's telephone was a contact number:

"In case of accident please notify: Tom Fielding, husband."

*

He had said goodbye to her that morning, stepping round the patches of ice on the path. He'd glanced up at the shutters, thinking they'd soon need another coat of white paint. The road curved down towards Greville Place, past the blocks of flats: on one side the modernised building with the huge arched window, and across the road, the dreary 1930s block, grandly called Greville Hall. At the main road Tom found a taxi and settled into the back seat to prepare for his mid-day meeting.

She would have taken the same route, only for some reason she had crossed the road between the zebra crossing near the Marriott

Hotel and the traffic island opposite Greville Place. She loved to tell him how she'd been to The Orient; the exotic name for their local 24-hour store, faintly grubby inside, selling everything from fish fingers to Middle Eastern wonders. She would come home with syrupy pastries, a pomegranate or a puffy flat bread. When she didn't want to cook they'd look in the freezer chest and make a meal of deep fried filo cigars or meat stuffed kibbe. If he could persuade her to entertain—which was rare—he'd buy the Turkish delight, the one with pistachios, nesting in a snow of sugar.

That day, she'd crossed the road and been hit full force by a car winging round the gentle curve where the congestion of Kilburn opens out into the wide pavements and trees of Maida Vale. A policeman had used her mobile phone to call Tom at his meeting and he'd rushed back to find the ambulance already gone. Half an hour after the crash he stood at the spot, still cordoned off and manned by two officers in day-glo jackets. There was a patch of blood in the road and the wind was whipping through the trees, knocking down the snow that had settled on the branches a day before. He stood there, unable to form the words that would ask which hospital she was in. An arm clothed in stiff yellow fabric was round his shoulder and the policeman was leading him to the other side of the road into a cafe.

"Have a cup of tea, sir, then we'll take you to St. Mary's."

At the counter, Tom looked at the pile of polystyrene cups and the packets of white bread.

"No thanks, I'd rather go straight away."

He didn't remember getting in the car, but as it built up speed, he looked up at a sign at the side of the road:

'Welcome to Westminster'.

CHAPTER 2

Tom joined the queue in the hospital cafeteria. A sign pointed to The Canal Restaurant, a name that conjured up locks and grassy banks. There was no failure in trade description—the cafe did overlook the canal that stretched as far as Camden—but the wall of window revealed buildings with crumbling paintwork reflected in a pool of grey. The designer who chose the pale wood tables was certainly not the same one who opted for the moulded plastic chairs. Over it all hung a smell of reheated food but in the late afternoon there was little to choose from. Warm metal containers lay empty and only the grill section offered the consolation of anything hot. Battered fish and fried chicken stood in ranks next to unidentifiable brown cubes—probably the vegetarian alternative.

Tom paid for his tea and walked past the empty tables to a stool by the window. Next to him was a young man drumming his fingers on a pack of cigarettes.

"Not much of a view, is it?" asked Tom.

"Eh?"

"The only good thing is that office block, though I wouldn't want to work in a glass box."

"Eh, certainly."

Tom sat down and put his drink on the counter. He'd overfilled the paper cup and some tea splashed over the edge. He glanced at the man. He was about his age—perhaps a year or two younger, in his late twenties. He looked as if he'd been out the night before, but for some reason had slept in his clothes. The striped cotton shirt was crumpled, half tucked into a pair of good jeans. The leather brogues had a layer of dust over a high polish achieved by constant buffing. Tom wondered whether to continue the conversation.

"You're Italian, no?"

"Eh" came the reply.

The man didn't look at him and kept opening and closing the lid of the cigarette pack. Then he turned his head and said:

"How do you know?"

"I don't know, the way you said 'certainly'—you meant 'certo'. I've travelled a lot in Italy."

He thought it would be rude to say that he could tell the difference between clothes that came from Zegna or Gap.

"Ebbene."

The young man thought his one-word responses would end the exchange. He was wrong.

"This isn't exactly Venice, is it? I've been there. I am in the art business."

"OK."

Tom looked at the man's long fingers, noticing that his nails were clean and carefully cut, straight across. Neither of them spoke. Tom sipped his tea, not bothering to mop up the pool on the counter. A sepia drop spattered on his laundered cotton shirt. The man stared out of the window. Tom looked at the uncombed hair and the heavy stubble on his dark skin. The silence between them settled on the tea, getting cold and sour in the paper cup.

"I hope you don't mind, only I'm waiting—waiting for news and it's nice to talk to someone."

"I don't—eh, I ... I'm waiting too."

"What do you do?" asked Tom.

"What do I do? I play piano."

"No I mean, what do you do for a living?"

"What I say, I play piano."

"Oh, you're a concert pianist? That sounds impressive."

There was no response so Tom continued in a nervous tumble:

"Are you famous? Do you play at the Barbican, the Festival Hall? I bet you've got some stories to tell about conductors."

"Not really."

"Not really what? the famous bit, or the conductors?"

Not answering either question the man muttered:

"I'm Joseph. Joseph Maggiore. But you won't have heard of me. I play Mozart. And Beethoven."

He looked at the tea-stained man and waited. Then the conversation started again:

"What's it like, when you've finished a piece and you look round the hall, with the audience applauding?"

"It's ... I don't know. I can't tell you."

"And do you play from music or do you remember it all?"

"In general I have the piece in my head."

The stilted English concealed what was going on in Joseph's mind. He didn't say that he practised every day and worked for four or five hours, that the notes were in front of his eyes and he felt them. When his fingers touched the keyboard they knew the sequence, exactly where to move.

They lapsed into silence again, but this time it was warmer, less hostile. The cafeteria was beginning to empty. Joseph got up.

"I have to get back ... my wife ... she's pregnant. She's in a coma. I need to be with her."

Wishing the man would stay Tom burbled on:

"My wife is unconscious too. She had an accident. She was crossing the road. She didn't see the car."

"I'm sorry, I have to go."

Joseph got up and walked out of the cafeteria. He made his way to the next building and took the lift to the Intensive Care Unit on the third floor. He nodded at the senior nurse who'd let him in and walked across the square room to a bed in the corner. Carla's eyes were closed, covered by tape. A thin sheet lay across the curve of her belly. In spite of the heat in the room her lower legs were enclosed in space boots, made from lamb's wool. Joseph tried to remember the conversation with the doctor on his first visit, six days before, as he stood staring down at his wife's motionless body. She was covered with pads connected to tubes. By her side was a series of monitors that flashed and beeped, but everything looked blurred through the glaze in his eyes. The doctor had tried to explain:

"The arterial line measures the blood pressure and concentration of oxygen and carbon dioxide in the blood."

"I see."

His eyes were wet. He couldn't take it in. The man in the white coat was still talking, pointing to the various tubes, explaining about a CVP line and what that was measuring.

"Never mind. I'll give you a fact sheet. You can't be expected to remember all this the first time. But it does help you to know what we're doing."

Joseph had taken the printed booklet and sat down by Carla's bed, going over the events that had started with a stomach ache and ended with his wife in a coma. It had begun the week before when she complained of an acute pain. It moved from her abdomen to her back. And then the vomiting began. Carla was in an agony that left her moaning and turning, writhing on the floor and begging him to do something. Without waiting for a doctor he decided to call a taxi and go straight to the hospital. They were directed to a cubicle where Carla kept a hand clamped to her mouth, trying not to cry out as the pain reached a crescendo of intensity. The doctors in Casualty seemed baffled. Carla was desperate for a painkiller and eventually a pethidine injection provided some calm. They sent her home. Two days later she was back again, the grinding, pumping pain soaring from her back to her stomach. A consultant finally came up with a diagnosis: pancreatitis.

Joseph found it hard to remember at what stage he'd been told that Carla had developed secondary diabetes. It was all a blur. Was it that the pancreatic tissue responsible for the production of insulin had been destroyed by the diabetes or had that caused the breathing problems, the three days of vomiting and the threat of kidney failure? Whatever the cause, Carla was in a coma, her pregnant belly the only part of her body not pierced by a tube or covered by a patch.

The nurse sitting at the end of the bed nodded to him:

"Is it beginning to make sense?"

"What you're doing, or why it happened?"

Joseph didn't expect an answer. He opened the booklet and turned to the section on Coma. It would have been hard enough to understand in Italian; terms like 'lung drainage', 'kidney function' and 'drip feed' were far outside his knowledge of English.

He stood up and walked round the bed. The nurse had told him to keep talking to her but what could he say? He leaned over and tried to whisper in Carla's ear. His throat was dry and mumbled words formed in his mouth but refused to come out. 'Amore' and 'tesoro' turned into a groan. He squeezed her hand, willing her to respond. All the time he was thinking:

"I'm sorry, I'm so sorry."

Joseph wiped his face with the sleeve of his sweater. At home he would have had an ironed handkerchief, laid out with every shirt Carla laundered for him. As he sat at her bedside, feeling guilty and irritated, he remembered her moody silences, alternating with over-bright chattering. Reliving the events that had brought her to the hospital, he knew he had no reason to link her present condition to the way he'd behaved.

He turned and left the room, rushing for an exit where he could have a cigarette and steep himself in sadness at his own stupidity. On his way out he bumped into a tall young man. Joseph lifted up his head and caught a glimpse of slightly thinning fair hair, a long nose and a pointed chin. He was the man from the cafeteria.

"Is your wife? Are they both in there?"

Tom nodded.

"Yes. They brought her here after the accident. I don't know about you, but I can't take it for long—looking at all those tubes and monitors."

They passed through the swing doors and Joseph rushed on ahead.

*

Tom was walking slowly, unsure of whether to go back to the cafeteria or to stay by Sophie's side. He thought it may be an hour or so before she woke up. The doctors had been noncommittal but the good news was that she was stable. From external appearances she seemed to be undamaged by the shock of the collision. There were no cuts on her face. The blood he'd seen on the road must have come from a gash on her leg. A junior doctor was approaching.

"Mr. Fielding, will you come with me for a moment."

Tom had hoped that he'd walk past and a voice inside was saying:

"It's not me he wants."

Inside the Visitors Waiting Room, Tom looked at the empty chairs but kept standing.

"This won't take long. He'll say it in a minute and then I can go in."

The doctor was running his fingers through his hair, fiddling with the stethoscope round his neck. He looked as if he were newly qualified. Or maybe he was still in the middle of his training, midway between gynaecology and paediatrics. He'd probably done six months learning about heart disease and spent time on the surgical wards. They must have taught him about diagnosis and disease, treatment and post-operative care. But he didn't seem to know about talking to the families.

"Why doesn't he just come out with it? She's shown some sign of movement and they need me to go and talk to her, play her familiar CDs, bring in her favourite perfume."

"Mr. Fielding. Your wife ... I'm afraid."

The doctor looked away from the husband's eyes, fingering his pager, willing it to ring.

Tom didn't need to hear the words. He suddenly felt sorry for the doctor. They hadn't taught him how to deliver bad news.

In the silence that followed Tom couldn't tell where the sounds were coming from. Had the doctor spoken or were they in his mind?

"I'm sorry. She's dead."

"Sorry?"

The doctor was speaking again, in a low mumble. He had probably said: "We did everything we could."

What Tom heard was a confusion of consonants; the words didn't matter. The meaning was clear.

CHAPTER 3

He must have been there a while, sitting on the cruel plastic seat. Someone was coming towards him—a nurse handing him a large paper bag. He held out his hand and took it; looked up at the ceiling, forcing his eyes open and his lips together. He wiped away the film of liquid that blurred his vision and put the bag down on the seat next to him.

The nurse was saying something:

"The police still have her filofax, but the phone is there."

Tom picked up the brown bag and began to tug at the staples. Inside was a Gucci handbag. He knew the name of the designer because Sophie had given him a lengthy explanation of the diamond pattern where each point had two Gs. You needed a magnifying glass to read the 'Made in Italy' under the name on the silver tag. He could hear her breathless voice, telling him the difference:

"It's not like Prada where the logo is large. And it's not as obvious as Louis Vuitton. Gucci is so refined."

He flipped down the leather handles and opened the zip. Inside was a muddle of keys, pens, tissues and a lipstick. Tom opened the lipstick, twisted the base and looked at the red slope. Sophie used to slick it over her lips without a mirror. He rolled it down again and put it in his pocket; unzipped the side compartment of the bag and taking out the silver Nokia, ran his fingers over the numbers. Then he got up, leaving the handbag on the seat. He looked at the mobile phone in his hand, hesitated for a moment and hurled it into a bin.

A porter turned his head, hearing the metallic crash. Tom was glad the thing had gone. A flash of guilt crossed his mind. In that one action he had turned the first of Sophie's possessions from a valued object into an item of no importance. He glanced back at the bin and walked on into the corridor past a row of six empty hospital beds, lined up like a train going nowhere.

*

Tom walked up the stairs and opened the front door. The flat was immaculate. It was the upper floor of an elegant house, on the edge of Maida Vale. At first they'd wondered if it was too near the pubs and market stalls of Kilburn but Sophie had looked at the hotel that formed the divide between the two and considered it trendy. It was quite usual to see a minor pop star emerging from a limo and disappearing inside the revolving doors.

The furnishings were his choice—a neutral palette of beige offset by dark wood and a single black leather chair. He had shipped over the chocolate grained chests and bookshelves direct from a showroom in Milan.

"Cream, beige and cinnamon. That's what we'll have."

It was more a stipulation than a suggestion and Sophie had agreed to the theme without argument. She was allowed to buy a coloured throw for the bed but no cushions and certainly no house plants.

"Yuccas are so seventies. We don't need any greenery."

Sophie had come to appreciate good taste in flowers. There was a time when she would come home with a bunch of mini chrysanthemums and four pink carnations. The first time the vase disappeared—only to find its way into the bathroom with one of the pink blooms removed—she didn't seem to mind.

Tom was gentle in his criticism:

"You have to have three or five, darling. Odd numbers. And really it's better just to stick to white."

From then on he ordered the flowers. She just needed to buy a tall vase, deep enough for a single white allium, Casablanca lilies or a mass of chincherinchees, a splash of bleached milk against the cream of the walls. Tom was trying to recreate a style that he'd seen many times in hotels all over Europe. It was his job to buy artwork for the bedrooms, dealing with students and established artists and selling their work to the hotel owners. He liked being an intermediary, encouraging creative talent and passing it on to an appreciative audience. Others might have seen his role in a different light. To bring the price down he told the artists they were lucky to sell multiple works. To justify his profit, he persuaded the hotel owners they were privileged to be party to nurturing such talent, which, of course, came at a price.

When he surveyed the hotel rooms, they were never occupied. So there were no unmade beds, no clothes strewn on chairs and the only books were the Gideon bible and a hard-back guide to the local shops and restaurants. In his own home Tom was trying to emulate this perfection, choosing clean lines of chrome and porcelain in the bathroom and white towels that needed daily replacement. Sophie had laughed that he'd soon expect her to fold the end of the toilet roll into a triangle.

Now the decor that had always given him such pleasure looked for the first time stark and colourless. He eased off his shoes, sank into the pale leather sofa and closed his eyes. Perhaps he'd been hard on Sophie. Did he give her enough say in what they bought or how they lived?

Before they'd moved in together Sophie had a collection of small objects that filled her student bedroom: shells from beach holidays, a shiny buddha that brought her comfort when she rubbed its tummy, and most precious, a carved mahogany elephant from the gift shop of the Hindu temple in Neasden. Tom had bought her an antique cigar box to keep them in. She had returned his generosity with hours of thought, culminating in a gift that he was sure to like. When he opened the box his fingers picked at the sellotape so that the wrapping paper could be carefully refolded without being torn. Inside was an Alessi pepper mill, a tall sculptural object made from fine beech.

There was no doubt that Sophie was happy. She had the time to pursue her interests and money in the bank to buy herself whatever she needed. With each new item of clothing in its pristine bag there would be a small gift for someone else. She would pack up a leather purse for one of her sisters or a boxed pen set for her father and post them off with a scribbled note that said "It's Tuesday and I thought you'd like this."

Tom didn't interfere. His mind was filled with work and he could see no harm in his wife spending money that came easily. The only arguments they had were about minor issues—like the ugly turquoise toothbrush that had to be replaced with something less gaudy. She finally agreed on matching white and grey electric toothbrushes standing like sentries on the bathroom shelf.

Tom pressed his finger on the door of a cabinet and it sprang open to reveal several bottles of single malt. He took out the Balvenie, poured a measure of the whisky into a crystal tumbler and leaned back again on the sofa. He waited for the usual pleasure of the complex flavour, but rolling his tongue round his mouth after the first swallow, found only a metallic aftertaste. He set the glass down on the table and almost immediately picked it up and walked into the kitchen.

The steel and granite surfaces were as bare as ever, save for a half eaten apple on a folded paper towel. He opened the fridge and pushed aside a couple of yogurts. He remembered a discussion about the words on the pack: 'Be kind to yourself'. How was Sophie being kind to her body by depriving herself of good food? While he enjoyed fresh pasta and artisan cheeses, she would make a lunch out of half a bag of washed salad and the thin, low-fat yogurt. He got out a plate and set it down on the worktop, breaking the cold silence around him. He unwrapped the waxed paper, cut a wedge of cheddar and finished it in two bites, leaving the plate unused.

The bedroom door was open. On top of the duvet was a crimson throw, in a soft material Sophie called chenille. He remembered the day she brought it home, arranged it on top of the white sheeting and called out:

"Come and look. It's like cranberries on snow. Say you like it."

"It's OK. It's a bit bright. Didn't they have it in russet or ..."

"Tom, you're impossible. I think your mother must have fed you too much chocolate or mashed potato. You can't appreciate anything that isn't beige or brown."

"That's not the point. We're aiming for a theme here. I'm not sure that red is at all right."

Sophie leaned over and moved the throw to her side of the bed.

"Fine, I'll keep it out of your way."

But of course it stayed. And there it was like a gaping cut in a finger, a gash of unwelcome red. On top of the throw were two designer bags. One had the name 'Laurel', the other 'Ferragamo.' Each of them contained a pair of black trousers. It was a sight so familiar that he hardly even noticed. Whenever he came home there would be new bags, bearing items that Sophie couldn't resist. Her wardrobe was full: jackets from Joseph, cashmere sweaters, a few outrageous tops from Christian Lacroix and floating skirts by Nicole Farhi. Tom flicked through the hangers—waiting to hear her voice:

"This one is different. Can't you see, Tom? It's not the same black—and the cut, can't you see it's special?"

What worried him was not the expenditure but the apparent waste. Sophie didn't wear the clothes. She seemed unable to stop buying, yet the pleasure never went beyond arranging them on padded hangers. She only wore a new outfit when they went out. For the rest of the time she was happy to wear the same black jeans and polo sweater. And yesterday, what was she wearing under the shearling coat, when the car had come sweeping into her path and knocked her into the air? He'd never know. He wasn't there when they cut through her clothes; when they lifted her into the ambulance and drove away.

The silence hung over everything; not the kind when they used to sit together leafing through magazines. This wasn't a gentle silence; it was aggressive and permanent. He felt it everywhere he went in the flat. He undressed and went into the shower, letting the hot water boom down on his body, drowning out the quiet. When he came out, he could hear it again, the stillness, the absence of that other body. Tom wrapped himself in a towel and wiped away the condensation from the mirror. He looked at his reflection and ran his hand over bottles of cleansing cream, eye make up remover and moisturiser. Then with a sweep of his arm, he sent the bottles crashing to the floor. He stepped over a pool of liquid and broken glass. Sophie might have laughed, saying 'It's lucky. It's white. It could have been worse.'

Tom dressed quickly, sank down in the leather Barcelona chair and remembered how they'd argued over its outrageous £1,000 price tag. He put his feet on the stool, pulled a folded handkerchief from his trouser pocket and wept.

Chapter 4

Joseph was standing in a small room, off the main ward, waiting to see the consultant. When he arrived, he stretched out a hand, indicated a chair and began the stream of words that was meant to make everything clear. To explain pancreatitis he began to talk about digestive enzymes and intestines.

But Joseph picked up only one word in four, so what he heard made no sense. The doctor went on:

"Let me explain. Your wife is having breathing problems. This is because the cells and tissues aren't getting enough oxygen."

He must have said more, but Joseph only took in the last two words 'lung failure'.

There was a pause and Joseph got up to leave. The consultant asked him to sit down again.

"Mr. Maggiore. We also have to consider the baby. Carla is twenty-eight weeks pregnant now."

"I know, of course."

"That means the baby is viable."

"What is 'viable'? You know my English is not so good. I don't understand this."

"Let me put it like this. The baby could survive if it were born tomorrow. But we don't want that. Every day in the womb, rather than outside, gives the baby a better chance."

The consultant didn't say that each day in the womb would be equivalent to a week with the staff dealing with infections and struggling to maintain the baby's breathing.

Joseph put his hand in his pocket, feeling for his cigarettes.

"I need to have a smoke. Can we talk about this tomorrow?"

"I don't think you understand."

It was always difficult talking to the families. The consultant decided to try again:

"Mr. Maggiore, we've had to put your wife into a drug-induced coma. This is to stabilise her. But I have to tell you, she is seriously ill."

"I've seen her. You don't need to tell me that."

"What I'm trying to say is this: In her condition. there is little chance of saving both her and the baby." He looked down and then added:

"And there is a considerable chance that we may lose both of them."

Joseph stared at him and felt a rush of words to his brain. The English whirled around with the Italian, with neither of them able to find a way out.

After what seemed like minutes, he spoke:

"So, what can you do? She can't have the baby if she's in a coma."

"There have been cases where a caesarian has been done. We adjust the drugs to include an anaesthetic and then we make an incision and remove the baby."

"But this sounds like a big operation," said Joseph.

"It's surprisingly short. It takes minutes."

The doctor didn't think it necessary to describe the procedure. He was picturing himself cutting through the layers of tissue to get to the uterus. He'd never done the operation on a comatose woman. He could imagine bringing out the baby's head, with the rest of the body sliding out. The operation usually took thirty minutes, including the stitching. In this case he'd be wise to try to speed it up.

"But we need your permission for this."

Joseph looked flustered. What was the doctor asking of him? Did he have to make a choice?

"You don't have to make a decision immediately. Carla's condition is serious but stable. The baby's heart beat is regular. We could wait a few days, but we couldn't consider waiting for weeks."

"What if I don't agree? Will Carla have a better chance?"

"Let's put it like this. At the moment it's not the pregnancy that is causing the problems. It's the lungs."

The doctor found it hard to deal with the husbands: the three-day stubble and the crumpled clothes. He needed to get back to his patients. The ones in intensive care didn't ask questions. Joseph turned his back and left the room.

He walked down Praed Street to the tube. He bought a newspaper and noticed the date: January 7th—one week since Carla had been rushed to St. Mary's Hospital. If only she'd been taken to King's College in Denmark Hill, it would have been so much easier. But they'd wanted her to be seen by a specialist who was unavailable south of the river. As he changed trains, he cursed the daily journey from Paddington to Kennington.

They lived in a road called Braganza Street. When they had first arrived in London, having moved from a small town in Tuscany, he told Carla that Westminster Abbey must be in the middle of the capital. They bought a map and wondered if there was anywhere they could afford within the square that made up Central London. They laughed at the names of the roads, 'Harmsworth' and 'Gaza', and finally settled on Braganza Street as the Italian name appealed to them and it was near the tube. They were lucky to find a ground floor flat to accommodate the piano, but when it was unloaded from the van, the removal men tutted as they measured the door frames. They left the piano in the rain, covered with an old blanket, while pedestrians skirted round it and Joseph ran to find a carpenter to take off the doors. Eventually the movers heaved the piano on to its side and slithered it into the front room.

*

Joseph reached into his pocket for the key and found that his hand was shaking as he tried to put it into the lock. Inside the doormat was littered with leaflets for local take-aways. There were dirty cups in the sink and piles of newspapers on the floor. Carla had never been tidy and he was used to living in a haze of clutter. She would leave her clothes on the unmade bed and she seemed unable to put away the half empty packet of pasta from the previous night's dinner. His mind was going over a typical conversation:

"Amore, please. Please to clear up a bit."

"What's the point?" asked Carla. "It'll be just the same tomorrow. I move this cup, you put down another one."

"Well at least take your things off this shelf."

Joseph swept a pile of letters off the window-sill.

"I've got to have somewhere to keep my music."

Carla stamped out of the room, her high heels clacking on the floor. She came back with a cardboard box and started to fill it with Joseph's things: his diary, notes and sheet music.

After that day he tried not to notice the chaos, the mass of jumble, the muddle of their lives. In the same way he refused to confront the state of Carla's mind. At first she had been excited about the move to London. She'd made an effort with the language, repeating new words she'd learned while they sat over bowls of bean soup, keeping out the winter. She'd lean over his plate and pick out a sprig of thyme, trying out a sentence: 'the cabbage is not black, like in Italy.'

They should have been settling down better. As Carla's English improved she became more confident but with a new vocabulary came a chattering that Joseph found irksome. He had no quarrel with what she was telling him; he was irritated by the constant interruptions. His days were spent in solitude, with no one speaking; his music only punctuated by the click of the metronome or the playback button of the recording machine. It's surprising that a concert pianist doesn't forget how to speak altogether; there is no dialogue during the hours of practising and in concert he says not a word, bowing as he takes his place and adjusts the stool. In the darkened hall he is concentrating on the notes, filling the minds of his audience with a kaleidoscope of sound, constantly forming new images and patterns.

It was some time before Joseph noticed the change in Carla's mood. Whereas before she had seemed content, her expression had now changed and a mist of depression hung over her, colouring her days a heavy grey. He wasn't sure when it had started—whether it was when he went away to play in foreign cities, or even before that, when he was trying to get established in London, playing in church halls and only rarely getting an assignment on a programme with a successful artist.

When he came home his wife was sullen and he became used to clipped conversations, even secretly welcoming mealtimes that were undemanding. As he closed the piano lid the final chords were still in his fingers; the notes still in his head. At first he thought nothing of their brief exchanges:

"You OK?"

"Yes. I don't go out today."

"But why not, Carla, it would do you good."

"Where's to go?" She looked mournful.

"You could come with me, to the concerts."

"Why? I hear the music here."

As the months wore on he recognised the signs of anxiety. Joseph could have dealt with a wife suffering from a heavy cold. He would have brought her hot drinks with a slice of lemon, popped out pills from a pack of paracetamol. If she'd had backache he could have given her a massage and whispered in her ear until the pain had gone and they were both on the bed together. But Carla was suffering from a pain inside her head; not the type that could easily be cured by medication; a pain that began when she woke up and stayed with her through cloud-filled days.

And now the curtain had come down and Carla was in the dark, thinking who-knows-what black thoughts as she lay in hospital, immobilised by the drugs. Joseph poured water into the base of his Moka Express, spooned in the ground coffee and screwed on the metal top. He left it on a high heat, knowing it would be two minutes before the puffing and bubbling announced that the coffee was ready. That would give him just enough time to settle himself at the piano and find the sonata he was working on.

It wasn't on the shelf or in the cardboard box where Carla had stuffed some of his music. He riffled through several Mozart scores but couldn't come up with the one he'd marked with scribbles and pencil notes.

"Where d'you put it Carla? I can't find it anywhere."

It wasn't her fault. She rarely moved any of his things. If he could just calm down, he'd remember where he'd put it. He walked over to the CD player and inserted a disc of Glenn Gould playing the Goldberg variations. Joseph began listening to the 14th variation, a hand-crossing whirlwind ending in brilliant cascades. It lasted a brief fifty nine seconds. He'd read about how Gould had achieved such an extreme tempo: he used to soak his hands and arms in hot water for twenty minutes before sitting down at the piano. For lesser players the key was to set the metronome to half speed and crank it up a notch every day. For him to achieve Gould's speed and dexterity would take hours and hours of practice. If the crispness of this fingerwork was supposed to cheer him up, it had the opposite effect.

He poured out the coffee and turned down the sound. As soon as he'd drained the cup he picked up his phone. He punched in a number and waited. His hand was shaking slightly. There was no reply. He left no message.

CHAPTER 5

Joseph was in a heavy sleep, dreaming that a phone was ringing and he couldn't find it. The ringing continued. He woke up and scrabbled among the pile of clothes he'd left on the chair. The noise was coming from the floor. The phone had fallen off the chair into his shoe. He picked it up and answered 'Pronto'. A voice at the other end was telling him to come to the hospital immediately. It wasn't what he was expecting.

"Your wife, she's started to have contractions. The baby is coming."

"But I thought ..."

"Just come, Mr. Maggiore. It won't be long."

He glanced at the clock. It was six o'clock and still dark outside. He pulled on the same clothes as the day before and threw a scarf round his neck. He'd never got used to this infernal climate—the wind and the rain. It was one of the things Carla hated too, but for her the main complaint was the grey sky that stretched from November to March with no relief.

He slammed the front door, rushed to the end of the street and as he turned right for the station, changed his mind and picked up a passing cab. It was only when he was slumped on the back seat checking for cash in his wallet that he realised he'd forgotten his keys.

There was little traffic at that time of the morning, even over the bridge and around Victoria. The taxi drew up at St. Mary's just before six thirty. Joseph rushed to the Intensive Care Unit and was told that Carla was in another building, in the delivery room. He stood in front of a board, scanning the names of the wards and departments: Bed Managers, Cardiothoracic, Cardiovascular, Coronary.

A passing student offered to show him the way to the delivery room. As Joseph stepped out of the lift he recognised one of the doctors from the Intensive Care Unit.

"Ah, Mr. Maggiore."

"What's happening. Is Carla having the baby? How is it possible? She's in a coma."

"Please. Sit down." The doctor indicated a chair and began to explain:

"It's very rare for a comatose patient to go into contractions, but this is what has happened."

"But I thought you wanted her to hang on."

"We did, but once the contractions started we just have to consider the best way to deliver the baby. Your wife is in an advanced stage of labour."

Joseph was edging past the doctor:

"I want to see her. I want to go in."

"You can't. Not at the moment. You'd be in the way. We'll tell you as soon as we know anything."

Joseph sat down and for the first time since Carla had been taken ill, he didn't reach for his phone. He leapt up every time a figure appeared and then sat down again, staring at his fingers. He began to move them, in a slow ripple, as if they were dancing over a keyboard. The swing doors opened and a figure in a green cotton suit came out, pulling off his mask.

"Mr. Maggiore, you have a baby boy."

Before Joseph could reply the doctor continued:

"I don't want you to get a shock. He's very small. It looks like he weighs just under a kilo. He's going straight to the special baby unit. You can come and see him in a while."

He disappeared and Joseph waited, unaware of what was going on. He couldn't see the nurse and paediatrician easing the baby into a plastic bag, fixing tubes, adjusting oxygen. Joseph remained outside the room, feeling for his cigarettes, pushing the packet back inside his pocket. Having no idea of the cause of the delay he muttered to himself, keeping an eye on the closed door. With a rush of air it suddenly opened and a transparent box was wheeled into the corridor. Joseph dashed forward; a nurse put out a restraining arm.

"Just wait a minute, then you can see him. We need to get him fixed up to the monitors first. We have to check his heart rate and breathing."

"But how is he? Is he OK?"

"We can't tell you anything yet."

Seeing Joseph's face, the nurse touched his arm and said:

"He looks good so far. This one's going to be a fighter."

What evidence did she have for this comment? Her remarks were purely to calm him down. She knew the dangers facing a baby of that weight and gestation. Hidden from view the doctor was inserting a tube into the baby's nose to blow in air at a prescribed pressure. Had Joseph seen this, he would have been worried. But it was a good sign. The baby was breathing for himself; he didn't need a ventilator.

The first thing Joseph saw was an incubator with a screen on the right and three or four monitors on the top. Inside was something very small with tubes connecting it to the support devices. It didn't look like a baby. Babies had big heads, not related to the size of their bodies. They had plump arms, kicking legs, mouths that opened to cry. What he saw was a perfectly formed miniature; legs and arms no thicker than the black notes on his piano, the ribs visible under the chest, the toes curling, fingernails intact. The baby had wisps of brown hair, eyes tight shut and a mouth covered by a small mask. His head was the size of an apple.

The incubator was being wheeled away. Joseph thought of how a doll came in a box with coloured wrapping. Here was his baby in a clear plastic container. He stood there, unsure whether to follow or not. He walked into the delivery room. Carla was lying on the bed, still unconscious.

*

In his mind he re-ran the events leading up to her pregnancy. It wasn't as if it had been planned. They'd had no conversation about the right time to start a family. How could they have done, with Carla in a perpetual depression and the music dominating his daytime hours, filtering into his dreams? Joseph wiped his hand across his eyes and then stretched out to run his finger over Carla's cheek. The doctors were huddled around another bed. Joseph turned and walked away, down the stairs.

He had already changed trains at Elephant and Castle when he remembered he had no door keys—Carla was the only one who had another set. Were they in the flat or might they be in the handbag he'd grabbed that day when he took her into hospital? He took a chance and decided to go straight back to the Intensive Care Unit. At each of the eleven stations Joseph tutted. Back at Paddington he rushed into the hospital and explained to the staff on duty what he was looking for. At the side of Carla's bed was a small locker. Inside was the handbag with the keys.

*

After the birth Carla was moved out of the labour ward and returned to Intensive Care. For two days Joseph hardly moved from her bedside. Nurses came to ask him if he wanted to go and see his baby. How could he explain that he was a different man from the one who had walked the corridors and spent time in the cafeteria? Now he seemed unable to move, slumped in a chair, dozing or staring at the monitors. Carla's swollen belly was flatter under the sheet, but in other ways there was no change. Joseph spent his days coming and going, sitting and waiting.

If anyone had asked why he didn't do the normal thing—to go and be with his baby—he wouldn't have had an answer. It was a subconscious decision that it was better to keep his distance. The boy was going to die. Let it happen quickly. He didn't want to watch a day-by-day deterioration. A few days earlier he'd been childless—more or less by choice. Now he was the father of a tiny, perfect looking baby, but the doctors' words and the fear in his brain told him that the chances of survival were small. It would surely be better for him to slip away now before the attachment that had already begun had taken a hold on him.

Four days after the baby's birth Joseph came through the main hospital doors, in no hurry to stand by Carla's bedside. He passed the board showing the list of departments and without knowing why, suddenly turned back and found himself scanning the names for the Intensive Care Baby Unit. He finally located it—ICBU. He found the lift, got out at the 4th floor and walked along the corridor. He pressed the bell, gave his name and the door opened. No questions were asked. Inside he was handed a gown and shown to a sink with a disinfectant soap and another substance to put on his hands after washing.

"Don't touch the taps with your hands. Turn them on and off by pushing with your elbows".

He followed the voice into a room with three incubators but what he noticed first was a low beep, beep noise. It seemed to be coming from all round the room. The lights were dimmed but he could just make out that the babies were naked except for minute nappies and woollen hats. Joseph stared at the hats, imagining children playing in the snow. But then he looked back at the babies' exposed skin, translucent and pale. The thought of skating and snowballs wafted out of his mind. The babies all had stickers on their bodies with wires connecting them to monitors. Lights flashed on and off. On one of the incubators was a label "Baby Maggiore, male, born 8th January, weight 830g".

830 grams. What did that mean? A can of cannellini beans weighed about 400g. So two of them were the equivalent of this baby and that included the head, the limbs, all the organs, bones. Joseph stood transfixed by the side of the incubator. His head was

a muddle of worry and uncertainty with no fixed point to anchor the fear that was rushing through it. 'He is so perfect, so beautifully formed. But I'm going to lose him. He's not going to grow up to be like other babies who cry and suckle. Other parents have children; I'm going to have a memory.'

Joseph held out his hand and noticed that his longest finger was the same thickness as the baby's leg. He stretched forward and placed the tip of his index finger in the baby's palm. Tiny fingers tried to close around it but were too small to grasp it.

He didn't realise that a nurse was standing by his side. She began to explain that premature babies don't know how to swallow, so they are fed minute amounts of breast milk through a tube.

"Carla wanted to breast feed the baby."

"I know, but as it's not possible we're doing the next best thing."

Joseph was trying to imagine another woman breastfeeding his baby. The nurse continued to talk and then seemed to be waiting for him to comment.

"Mr. Maggiore, will you agree?"

"Agree, to what?"

"I was saying we have a supply of breast milk from the other mothers and that's what we'll give him, but we need your permission."

Joseph mumbled his consent and looked from the baby to the four monitors banked up beside the incubator.

He'd seen it all before in the adult intensive care unit, but there was one thing missing from the technology at each bedside: none of the machines registered what the patient was thinking. He imagined a string of thoughts being projected on the screen: 'I'm hungry, I'm tired, leave me alone.'

"I just want to show you something else, Mr. Maggiore. These leads on his chest. This one's checking his heart rate and the other goes to an apnoea monitor. It registers when the baby's breathing is irregular. An alarm sounds immediately and we come and deal with it."

Joseph picked up two words of this sentence, 'breathing' and 'irregular'—surely the same in Italian, irregolare. He asked what it meant.

"Well, he might actually stop breathing."

"O dio. That means he will die."

Joseph didn't know that premature babies often stop breathing for as much as fifteen to twenty seconds at a time.

"No, that's what I'm saying. The machine picks it up and we come straight away and he'll start again."

Instead of going into details, the nurse continued in a more cheerful voice:

"The woolly hat is to prevent heat loss—tiny babies lose a lot of heat through their heads."

Joseph couldn't take it all in. What came as the greatest shock was the panic he felt when he saw the little chest heaving. Just looking at the strands of fine hair peeping out from underneath the hat made his eyes cloud with tears.

The doctors were dealing with problems he couldn't imagine. He had only one thought: how could they save his baby? He'd read magazine articles about the instant love between a mother and a newborn child. Joseph was not prepared for the lurching in his stomach as he looked at 'Baby Maggiore male'. No-one had told him what he would feel when he watched his son, struggling to hold on to a fragile world, yet seeming to sleep calmly as though nothing was wrong. Joseph rushed outside, pulled on his gloves, poking at the hole in one of the fingers, and walked slowly in the cold January air. It was hard to believe that six months earlier his life had been filled with a strange excitement and a joy he thought would last for ever. Now he had a baby son who was struggling to survive—and his wife was in a coma.

CHAPTER 6

Tom woke to the sound of Jazz fm. He stretched a hand out of a thick sleep, turned off the radio and glared at the clock face projected in light on the ceiling. 9.35 am. After hours of lying awake, he'd finally succumbed to a pill-induced stupor. His thoughts seemed to click in automatically: 'I'm awake. Sophie's dead. Why get up?'

He heaved himself off the bed and went over to the flashing button on the answerphone. There were several messages. The first two were from art students and followed a familiar pattern. "I'm not really pushing you, and I know you're busy, but I wondered if you'd had a chance to consider my work." He'd made contact with two new artists recently. One had a portfolio of paintings in vertical stripes; the other had an idea for reproducing extracts from old local newspapers on linen. Both of them were waiting for a response. Tom listened to the third message. A voice was saying something incomprehensible. He clicked back, then forward again:

"This is the Steigenberger Frankfurter Hof."

Of course. Tom had been trying to book a hotel room in Frankfurt and they were calling to confirm. Usually the idea of work excited him and his mind could run on three or four tracks simultaneously. On one line would be the artists and their work; on a parallel line would be a list of hotels with bare walls. But today all Tom could think of was train lines merging; with him in charge of the points, unable to stop a fatal crash. Shaking his head to get rid of the image, he pressed the button again and groaned. It was Sophie's sister, Gemma:

"Tom, I've been trying to get hold of you. You said you'd confirm the arrangements for the funeral. Are you organising the cars or shall I do it? Get back to me."

The last message was from the police:

"Mr. Fielding. We need to come and talk to you again. Is it all right if we come at ten?"

Assuming that they meant ten in the morning, that left Tom fifteen minutes to shower and dress. He had no time to play the messages again and wondered if he'd missed one. He made sure not to press the delete button and walked into the bathroom.

There was no phone call from his mother, Caroline. He'd had a brief conversation with her on the day Sophie died and she'd offered to fly over but suggested it might be better for her to come after the funeral. How was it that this was no surprise? Or, more painful to confront, that his mother's presence at his wife's burial would bring him no comfort?

Caroline Fielding had been living in Spain since the death of Tom's father. She was a woman whose life had revolved around her husband. Unable to function on her own and with few friends, there seemed no reason to stay on in the house in Surbiton. After Tom had sorted out her finances they'd agreed that if she were going to move, it would make sense to live in a sunnier climate. She put the house on the market and studied property options on the Costa del Sol. A persuasive salesman told her about an English-speaking community near Marbella and convinced her to move to a newly built complex complete with patio doors overlooking the swimming pool. Caroline knew she'd never use the golf course. She had no interest in the yachts in the marina, but there was a store nearby that stocked baked beans and Marmite. She had sold the house in Surrey and left behind a few neighbours who would miss her pavement chatter. Only a handful of people had received a change of address card. There was no-one who had shared an intimate friendship, discussed the latest novel or seen beyond the fixed smile and the carefully applied make-up. A comfortable limousine ordered by Tom arrived to take her to the airport. Curtains twitched as Caroline drove away.

She made a point of having a weekly phone conversation with her only son. She fitted it in between a siesta and a game of bridge, filling him in on details of the hands she'd played and the BBC sitcoms she'd found on satellite TV. She reassured him that there was no need for her to learn Spanish. Tom told her about his travels, trying to interest her in the paintings he was buying or the architecture in Florence. He remembered trying to explain the problems of constructing the dome of the great cathedral in the fifteenth century.

"It took six years to complete. Can you imagine? They needed to raise stone and marble to the height of a multi-storey building. You know how they did it? They used a hoist, powered by an ox."

"Really, darling?"

"Then the architect arranged for food and wine to be taken up to the workers. He knew that going up and down hundreds of stairs would exhaust them. Mind you, the wine was diluted."

"Poor things."

The line went quiet.

"Are you there, mother?"

"Yes, darling. but I have to go. Can't be late for bridge."

Their relationship had never been close. At the age of eight Tom had been sent to boarding school and learned to control the tears that came at bedtime. He soon discovered the road to popularity: a love of football and the company of boys who kept away from the 'swots'. By the time he graduated to public school he had learned how to pass exams. There was no need to try to excel at anything; he needed to do just enough work to anticipate the questions and when his own knowledge was too sketchy to give a full answer he would drop his rubber and, leaning over to pick it up, glance at the paper of the boy at the next desk. At Prize Day he dreaded the arrival of his parents. His father, a Civil Servant in the Treasury, would engage his teachers in questions about his son's work, subtly reminding them that he was a man to be reckoned with, part of the backbone that made up the country's support for the political party in power. His mother stood by his side while they watched the sports, lifting a high-heeled shoe out of the grass and talking just that bit too loud. But it was her hair that was the real embarrassment: a deep red that would have been fine on a leaf in New England, but looked to him as if too much of the mixture had been stirred in, leaving a mane of over shiny colour, glinting wickedly in the sunlight. Tom kept his distance, sidling up to other families in the hope of meeting someone's sister or sharing a slice of fruitcake from a picnic hamper.

*

When the doorbell rang, Tom was zipping up his trousers. Thinking about his mother had slowed him down. He pulled a sweater over his shirt, went to answer the door and showed the officer into the living room. The policeman's boots seemed uncomfortable on the twisted pile carpet; the waxy anorak at odds with the pale sofa. Tom put the kettle on to boil, spooned coffee into the gold-rimmed cafetiere and got out a carton of milk.

"Like some coffee?"

"Yes please, sir. Two sugars."

Tom poured in the boiling water and waited a couple of minutes.

"Hope you like it strong," he said, squeezing the filter down through the black liquid.

"As it comes, Sir."

He poured milk from the carton, handed the mug to the officer and then, as he was putting it down, noticed that the cream had separated into circles of fat. He leaned over and took in the sour smell:

"Oh, God. The milk's off."

"Never mind. I already had a drink at the station."

They sat there, not talking, looking at the curdled globules rising to the surface.

"Mr. Fielding. Can we talk about the accident? Can we retrace your wife's movements before it happened?"

"I've told you. She was probably going shopping. She did most days."

Tom remembered a discussion they'd had the week before, when he suggested that Sophie's urge to buy fashionable clothes was getting out of hand:

"You could clothe all the women lawyers in London with the number of black trouser suits you own."

Sophie was quiet. She'd moved around a few hangers in her wardrobe and said, with a smile:

"Not quite. You don't see many barristers turning up to court dressed in Armani."

"But Sophie, it doesn't make sense. You bring the clothes home but you hardly ever wear them."

"You just miss the point, Tom. If you're a collector, you don't have to use the objects you collect. What about rare stamps? You don't stick them on letters. And coins? You don't keep them to put in parking meters."

She had won her point. He had no reply. The officer brought Tom's attention back to the accident.

"... why do you think that was?" he asked.

"Sorry, what did you say?"

"Why do you think she didn't cross at the zebra crossing. And if she was going into town, why had she crossed the road at all? The buses that way go towards Kilburn."

"I don't know. I expect she was going to The Orient. I've told you all this. She used to pop in there for things like olives and baklava. We ordered on-line for most of the stuff. I couldn't get the hang of it at first. I typed it all in—washing powder, loo paper, fizzy water—and then, when I'd done the whole list, the screen went blank and I lost it all. I had to start again. But now, it's a doddle."

"Yes, I believe it is, though I don't do it."

"They even remind you of things you ordered last time. And the delivery is OK too, you just give them a time slot and they bring it round. Some people don't like it though. They don't want a Tesco or Sainsbury van unloading outside their house. If it was Harrods it would be different."

"Mr. Fielding. Can we get back to the road?"

"I'm sorry. I didn't mean to go on like that."

His long fingers were pulling at the wedding ring.

"Your wife must have known it well—how it curves round and opens up, so the traffic coming round the bend speeds up after the lights and the hold-ups in Kilburn."

"Yes of course she knew it."

"Now this car that was coming ..."

"It could have swerved. A bus might have been overtaking on the other side. That's probably what happened. He swerved to miss the bus."

"Mr. Fielding. We've got a couple of witnesses. Neither of them mention a bus."

"Well then, he was just going too fast."

"They say the car wasn't speeding. One of them says your wife walked out into the middle of the road and the driver didn't have a chance."

Tom picked up the mug of cold coffee and took it into the kitchen. When he came back the policeman was looking at a notebook.

"... yes, here it is. 'The car was not going fast.'"

"But the road could have been slippery. It had been snowing," said Tom. "The driver should have slowed down."

"But we need evidence, Mr. Fielding. I have to say it again; neither of the witnesses mentioned that the car was speeding. To bring a court case we need to prove that the driver was at fault."

"Of course he was at fault. He killed Sophie."

The police officer put the notebook back in his pocket. How could he explain that without the evidence, they couldn't possibly prosecute the driver?

"Mr. Fielding. I know how hard this is for you. I know what you want, Sir. You want him off the road and never driving again."

"I didn't say that. I just want justice."

The policeman zipped up his jacket and began walking to the door. Over the years he'd helped to prosecute many traffic cases that involved an injury.

When they involved a death they were always more of a problem. Even if there was evidence of careless driving, the defendant would often leave court with little more than a fine. One particular case stuck in his mind. A sixteen year old boy had been killed by a car going at 35 mph. The magistrates filed out of court to consider their verdict, leaving groups of lawyers and police officers whispering and waiting. The family of the victim sat silently in the gallery. After ten minutes the three JPs returned and sentenced the driver to a short disqualification, nine points on his licence and a fine of £200. Everyone except the family was expecting this. The victim's mother glared at the bench and covered her mouth with her hand. How could it be right to equate her son's life with the price of an iPod?

But in this case there was no evidence of speeding; nothing to show that the driver was at fault. Could the woman have walked into the middle of the road, straight in front of him?

"Mr. Fielding. One more thing. Would you say your wife was happy?"

"What a ridiculous question. Of course she was. And she'd still be here now if this idiot hadn't killed her."

The policeman had his hand on the catch of the front door. He was looking for a way to end the conversation. He couldn't have chosen a more misguided comment:

"I ... I have to tell you something. We had the driver down at the station. He's in a bad way."

"Oh yes?"

"He hasn't been able to go back to work. He's quite devastated."
Tom stared at the officer and watched as he let himself out.

CHAPTER 7

Joseph went to bed with a toothache. Hours later it was still grinding away, spreading up the back of his jaw. By morning it had moved to his cheekbone. When the alarm went off, he grabbed the clock and put it on the floor, sliding it out of reach. Fifteen minutes later it rang again. Joseph staggered out of bed without opening his eyes and in an effort to reach the clock, stubbed his toe on the base of the bedside table. The pain was so intense that he immediately forgot about the toothache.

It seemed as if his brain couldn't deal with multiple problems. It was like pressing the keys of an old-fashioned typewriter. If you tapped two together, the type-bars jammed and the page was blank. So it was with pain and emotion. The throbbing toe had pushed out the agony of the toothache and the intense worry about Carla had been overtaken by the panic that he would lose his newborn son.

Joseph remembered Carla pointing out stories in the newspaper. "Can you imagine? 'Father and son drowned in seaside tragedy'?"

"No, I can't. I don't know why you read these pages. It's so depressing. And you're not feeling cheerful at the best of times."

"That's got nothing to do with it. I was just thinking how the mother must have felt."

Since the baby's birth he hardly read the papers at all and certainly never lingered over the 'human disaster' pages. Even looking at the headlines made his fingers shake as if the words on the page could transfer to his life and become reality.

In his daily visits to the hospital he stayed for hours by the incubator, only moving when the room was filled with doctors. When the procession moved on to the High Dependency ward next door, the nurses went back to the babies in their charge, adjusting the tubes, checking ventilation pipes and preparing syringes.

Joseph watched as the nurse flicked the switch that raised the top of the incubator. She lifted the baby to turn him to the other side and adjusted the soft bedding so he could curl up again. To an outsider it seemed as if his limbs were so fragile; so bone-thin. There was little flesh to round out the thighs; none of the plump creases between the hand and the arm of a normal baby. Yet his slender finger could withstand the pressure of a probe to monitor oxygen levels; the joints of a leg barely five inches long could bend without cracking.

The families visited at any hour of the day or night, so they passed each other in corridors, rarely meeting by the side of a cot. Joseph stood, often alone in the room, peering into the incubator, pacing up and down and eventually dozing in the chair to the rhythmic beat of the monitors.

At home he would dial the hospital number by the side of the phone. After a few days he no longer referred to the scrap of paper, but pressed the eight digits from memory. The call went straight through to the Intensive Care Unit. When the daytime team handed over to the night shift, information was passed on to deal with questions from anxious parents. The hours around midnight were the busiest. That was the time when a father would wake from a bad dream or a mother would imagine that her baby was struggling for breath.

"That's fine, dear. 'Course we don't mind. We're here all the time."

For Joseph it was crucial to know how much milk his son was taking. He had to start putting on weight.

"Hold on a minute, I'll go and find out."

"And what about his breathing. Did he stop?"

"Only once. See you in the morning, Mr. Maggiore."

But sometimes Joseph couldn't wait. He began to visit during the night. He found out that if he timed it right, he could catch a night train and arrive at the hospital in forty minutes. The lights in the unit were low, as they were during the day, and the activities continued round the clock. When the sun came up in the sky outside, the night staff passed progress notes on to the next team. On 17th January, nine days after the baby's birth, Joseph stood by the incubator waiting to see the neonatal specialist. There was a name on the label: 'Matteo Maggiore'—birth weight 830g.' Beneath that was a chart, and on that day his weight was entered as 750g.

"Ma, non capisco." Joseph had reverted to Italian: "I don't understand. Why is his weight going down?"

"He's not so well today. We've done some blood tests. He's got an infection. It's very common in these little newborns. What we're going to do is start him on some antibiotics until we get the test results through."

Joseph looked at Matteo. He'd chosen the name without Carla's permission. His cousin Marta had given birth to a son after four daughters and had called him Matteo. She told him it meant Gift of God. His Matteo had a bandage on his leg and a tube in his head. They'd had to shave his hair and the sheet was covered with downy strands. Joseph stood near, unable to speak.

The doctor continued:

"You probably want to know why he's got a bandage on his leg."

"What happened?"

"Nothing serious. It's because the fluid in the tubes carrying the medication sometimes leaks from the vein and causes the tissues to swell."

Neonatal doctors had a lot of experience of dealing with parents in shock. They argued over whether it was better to tell them everything, or simply to answer their questions. This one believed in full explanations.

"We've also put a drip in his arm and for the moment we've stopped feeding him. You've probably noticed that his eyelids seem a little sticky. That could mean an infection, so we're giving him drops into his eyes."

By this time there were five people standing round the incubator. Joseph left the room. When he came back Matteo's eyes were covered by a pair of white cotton goggles.

The doctor continued to explain every procedure:

"There's nothing to worry about. It's like when he had jaundice, in the first few days. I don't think you were here then, were you? They put on the goggles to protect his eyes from the phototherapy lights. If there is an infection it's better to keep him in the dark."

Every day there was another problem. He picked up parts of what the doctors said: 'possible heart murmur', 'a duct that might need medication to close it', 'the drip has slipped out of the vein, it's tissued and made the arm swell.'

And through it all Matteo lay curled up, with his chest rising and falling—the only sign that he was alive. He made no sound and never cried.

Carla's condition was unchanged. The doctors had told Joseph that she could be in the coma for another few weeks. He moved from Matteo's incubator to Carla's bedside and at each one he whispered about the other. Carla wasn't even aware that she'd had a baby but Joseph needed to tell her every detail of Matteo's progress, every setback.

Beneath it all was a feeling of guilt: the knowledge that he had caused Carla's misery. The thoughts racing through Joseph's mind actually made him feel queasy, as if all his worries were finding their way to his unsettled stomach.

Upstairs on the fourth floor a nurse was taking the tube from Matteo's head and inserting a new feed tube down his nose, all the while talking to him.

"Come on little one, it's dinner time, let's get this tube down— carefully now, it's got to go into your stomach."

She knew it would be a fatal error if the tube released even a few drops of milk into his lungs. The rhythmic beep of the monitors meant there was a rare moment of calm in the room. None of the babies was in imminent danger.

*

Joseph had somehow adapted to his new existence, settling into a routine of dejection interspersed with sudden moments of panic. At home he barely ate, but forced himself to play the piano in the hours when he wasn't phoning or lying restless in bed.

He was working on a Beethoven sonata with a concert date looming in February. His fingers moved over the keyboard, settling on too many wrong notes. Each time he began again, working through the Rondo, stumbling at the same few bars, until he slammed down the piano lid and picked up his mobile for the seventh time that day.

As he waited to be put through to the ICBU, the other phone started to ring. Maybe Carla was coming out of the coma? Maybe he could make everything right again? If only Matteo could survive, they could build a new life.

"No, I can't tell you anything on the phone. You need to come. I can't discuss your wife's condition. That's why we want to talk to you."

Joseph didn't recognise the doctor's voice. Perhaps it was an administrator. The medical staff were rarely as abrupt. He made sure his keys were in his pocket, closed the front door and walked down Braganza Street, not in any hurry. He stopped to pick up a pack of Marlboros at the station and was about to put the change in his pocket when a gust of wind swept him forwards, scattering the coins on the steps. In the hospital, he walked up the stairs to the fourth floor and passed through the swing doors. The curtains were drawn round Carla's bed. Inside there were sounds of movement, the wheeling of equipment, sharp instructions being issued. Joseph stood waiting. After a minute a young doctor emerged. He opened his mouth to speak and at that moment Joseph caught a look of embarrassment in his eyes. The young man looked tired, as if he'd been on duty long past his nine-hour shift. It was then that Joseph knew.

"Don't tell me. No. it's not true."

"Mr. Maggiore, the trauma of the birth—it was too much; her organs were failing."

"She's not. She can't be."

The doctor stretched out his hand in a calming gesture, but Joseph brushed it away.

"But you were keeping her alive. Why did you let her go?"

"We ..."

"You could have done something."

Several nurses had gathered round. Joseph heard someone say:

"I'll go and fetch the consultant."

Joseph grabbed at the doctor, pulling at his pale green jacket. And then he was glaring at his face, shouting and spitting out a barrage of words:

"Che cazzo, why wasn't I here? Why didn't someone tell me sooner? Why didn't you save her, porca puttana?"

Two other doctors led him to a chair. Someone brought a cup of milky tea. In the struggle it was knocked aside, a pool of sweet heat spreading over the floor and Joseph's feet tripping, splashing till he finally fell silent, his hands over his eyes, his elbows digging into his knees.

As suddenly as he'd lost control, he regained it and stood up. He walked back to the bed where Carla lay, the machines silent, a sheet outlining her mouth, with no breath to lift it above her face. He turned and left the room.

part two

BEFORE

CHAPTER 8

June 2001

Tom is carrying a breakfast tray. Propped up between the toast and the coffee pot is a surprise for Sophie's birthday: two airline tickets. Most people don't enjoy surprise parties—friends jumping out at you as you open the door—but the chance of a few days in Paris is another thing. Three days later they are settling in to the Hotel La Villa in rue Jacob, an elegant building on the Left Bank. Tom has been here before, on his own, in a room of masculine purple, but this time he's chosen a suite bathed in white and ecru, with modern lighting reflecting the brilliant walls.

This is the first time Tom has taken his wife on a working trip abroad. Sophie loves hotels. For him, they're just part of his work and the first thing he sees is what's on the walls. She revels in everything, folding back the bed cover to see how many pillows there are, clicking the remote on the TV, checking to see what goodies are in the bathroom. She keeps the hotel note pads and asks for replacement bottles of bubble bath. She eats croissants for breakfast, enjoying the change from her usual low-fat yogurt. Thoughts about weight and diet seem to disappear for a few days.

Sophie lifts the thick towelling robe off the hook on the bathroom door. She's reading a note on the hanger. Tom knows that it refers to the hotel shop where you can buy one. He knows she has no intention of buying the robe: she's far more interested in picking up the free miniatures by the bath. He believes she never had enough party bags when she was little.

Sophie snuggles down in the linen sheets. He is frustrated, that even now, after four years of marriage, she still doesn't like to undress in broad daylight. She's fingering the alarm clock and they exchange a few words about the timing of his meeting the next day. It would be natural for him to ask her how she's planning to spend her time but he doesn't want to risk another conversation about clothes and shopping.

Sophie has taken to buying designer clothes. First it was a Louis Feraud suit, then trousers from Agnes B. Lately her taste has changed and she's brought with her a suitcase full of asymmetric tops and dresses with uneven hems. As she was packing he'd asked:

"Sophie, are you going to wear any of these things?"

"Of course. This one is by Hussein Chalayan. He aims to transfer undesirables into desirables."

"Are you talking about people?"

"No, he's talking about restoring old clothes into fashionable new ones. At his London show he had a bodice and skirt made out of moulded sugar glass. At the end he deliberately smashed them to pieces."

Tom looks at some of the clothes.

"The names of these designers—Imitation of Christ—that's a label to put in a dress? And what about Planet Yumthing and Indigo People? I think they're actually pop groups that didn't make the charts."

"Don't laugh. Some people take them very seriously. Indigo People, for example, you're talking crunchiness with fitted tailoring; sci-fi geometric shapes with flying geese. These are clothes for loft living urban yuppies."

By this time they are both giggling. At least she sees the funny side of her obsession.

Paris should be the perfect break. Sophie is looking forward to shopping. She's excited about the glittering hush of the designer palaces on avenue Montaigne. A friend has told her about a 'seconds outlet' where you can buy 'the real thing' for far less. But apparently there's a problem: they remove all the labels so you can't take the clothes back and get free alterations from the designer shop. Sophie doesn't tell her friend that the whole point of the designer clothes is to show off the prestigious label.

Tom would like to tell their friends they have been on a glass covered boat on the Seine and climbed to the top of the Eiffel tower at night, but when he gets back from a day of meetings he's tired from the hours of negotiation and has little enthusiasm for anything more than dinner and an early night.

*

Ten months later they are in Antwerp in a small hotel, De Witte Lelie. There are just ten rooms in what was once two gabled houses from the 16th century. Everywhere is white, from the linen sofas and the eye-blinking walls, to the chairs and the bedding. Above the marble fireplace is an arrangement of white flowers—lilies, of course, after the name of the hotel. Sophie has slipped off her shoes on to the polished floor and is bouncing up and down on the bed:

"Tom, it's like ice cream—the white everywhere. When we get home we should get rid of the beige and grey and do our place up like this."

"The only place I'm planning to do up is the Corinthia."

"What's that?"

"Told you, it's the big hotel I'm working on. We passed it on the way here."

"Sorry."

"Sophie, are you listening?"

"Yes."

"It's the glass skyscraper." He hands her a brochure. She glances through it and laughs:

"This is a bit corny. Listen to this: 'The Corinthia sparkles like one of Antwerp's diamonds.'"

"All I know is that it's got 215 rooms, so it's good business for me."

"What kind of art are you buying for it?"

"Don't know yet. I've got three artists lined up."

"And they can produce that number of paintings?"

"That's what I want to find out. One of them does photographs — terrific snow scenes in black and white — and he can reproduce them in quantity. But I've got another artist who's doing abstracts made of crushed stone. Sophie, stop shaking the bed, you're making me feel seasick."

"So, it's black and white stone, right?"

"You're just not listening. I was talking about these artists. I won't even bother to tell you what the third one does."

"I'd go for the stone crusher. His work should fit in with your theme. Everything has to be sand-coloured, no?"

Tom checks his papers, picks up the room key and blows her a kiss:

"Got to go. I'll be back about seven. Where will you go while I'm out?"

"We're here for two days, right? Well, today I have to go to the Rubens House, but tomorrow ..."

"Don't tell me, it's shopping."

"Actually it's more than shopping. There's a Fashion Museum — avant-garde design."

Tom is relieved that Sophie finds it easy to keep herself happy while he's working. He spends most of the day in a meeting with the photographer. The price of the snow scenes is more than he wants to pay. But they are exactly the right shape to go on a wall behind a bed. And they're already on blocks so there'll be no need for frames. At six thirty he leaves the Corinthia and goes back to the Witte Lelie. He walks into their room, throws his folder on a chair and shouts:

"Sophie baby, I'm back."

She calls out from the bathroom: "Be out in a minute."

He reaches over to the antique table and pours himself a sherry from the glass decanter. The humming of the hair dryer means that she's shaking out her hair, blowing the heat through the dark strands till they go back to blonde. In the bedroom she pulls on a bias-cut black dress. Tom doesn't know the difference between chiffon and satin but he can see how it slides over her skin, clinging at the waist and barely touching her hips. He pulls her towards him from behind. She turns and moves her head. Bringing her eyes back to his face, she presses against him and allows their mouths to meet.

The next morning they come down to breakfast to find it laid out on a crisp white tablecloth. There are warm rolls, jams and freshly cut cheese.

Sophie picks up a slice of Gouda:

"Remember that hotel in Amsterdam? The one where they served up that vacuum-packed cheese? It was all damp and mouldy. This is a bit different."

Tom doesn't reply.

"Hey, you were there too, don't you remember?"

Instead of responding Tom wishes she didn't always see the negative side of things. She's always going over the past, while he can block it out. He could go for months without giving a thought to his parents; the sudden heart attack that cut short his father's life followed by almost daily conversations with his mother about life insurance, probate and the broken washing machine.

Sophie turns to ask the waitress something and before she can open her mouth, a pot of Assam tea and a jug of coffee are put down on the table.

"There you are." says Tom. "They even remember what we asked for yesterday."

As he pours the tea, he asks:

"So where is it today? Are you going to this Fashion Museum?"

"Yes. I've heard it's got a huge staircase and you can see the sky from the ground floor. You'd love it. Though I don't expect you're interested in Dries Van Noten and Ann Demeulemeester."

"Andy who?"

"Ann de ... you're doing this on purpose." Sophie looks exasperated. Tom stops spreading the butter on his roll and says:

"I was joking. These designers are all the same to me. Sophie, tell me something."

"What?"

"Tell me why you find shopping so exciting. Why do you want to have more and more clothes, when you hardly wear the ones you've got?"

"Don't let's start that again. I've told you. It's not just wearing them. It's finding them, looking for something different. You don't want me to look like all those women who shop at Jaeger or Burberry. They're so boring. Real design takes you somewhere. into another world."

"But what's wrong with the world we live in? I thought you liked it? The way our flat is done up, the friends we've got."

"I know where this is leading. It's about Alex and Vivienne, how we owe them an invitation."

Tom looks downcast. "I never said anything."

"You don't have to. You want me to make a dinner party."

"Well, now you mention it, there are people we should invite back, Peter and Ann, John and Jenny. But you don't have to cook. You could buy things from that shop, opposite, what's it called? The Orient. Buy the olives and pastries from there, and then go to a deli and get some fresh pasta or something."

"Tom, I don't want to be hassled. I don't enjoy having people to dinner. There's all that 'underconversation.'"

"What do you mean?"

"You know, the questions: 'What do you do?'—'I stay at home and don't work.' 'Where do your children go to school?'—'We don't have any.'"

"Now you're talking about something else. It's not the food at all, is it? It's kids. Why you don't want any."

"I just want you to understand."

"We've been through all this. Let's not start again."

Tom has heard it all before. How Sophie was a middle child. Her older sister Gemma got all the attention and her younger sister Debs was the baby.

"... they never had time for me. My father was so busy making Gemma feel 'special' and then Mum was fussing over the baby. You know she even insisted on breast feeding her in public. It was disgusting. I was so embarrassed."

"But Sophie, I'm not talking about having three children. We could just have a go and try it with one. That's assuming we don't have triplets first time."

Sophie isn't listening any more. She has a habit of changing the subject by refusing to respond. She's leafing through the catalogue of the Rubens House. She stops at a page and points to a self portrait of the artist.

"You know he got up at four in the morning. He could paint with all sorts of distractions going on. He could dictate a letter or carry on a conversation with a visitor and all the time he'd be putting the paint on the canvas. How many pictures do you think he painted?"

"Who?"

"I just showed you. Peter Paul Rubens."

Since he doesn't seem to have heard her question, she answers it herself:

"He did more than fifteen hundred paintings."

Tom is picking up his papers, pushing his plate away. In spite of wanting to get to his meeting he is thinking about Rubens and his surprising output:

"But he didn't do every brush stroke himself. He couldn't have done. He had pupils who would fill in the detail for him."

"Maybe that's why he had such a calm face."

Sophie is still looking at the self-portrait: "This picture of him. He's got that piercing look, so alert. I found out something interesting. Did you know he had two wives?"

"That's nothing unusual."

"No, listen. He was married to the first one Isabella for about seventeen years, then after she died he married again. He was fifty-five and his new wife Helene was only sixteen."

Tom wonders where this is leading. Sophie carries on:

"He put the two wives in a painting, together. That was odd, wasn't it?"

"There you are. He probably wanted another child and couldn't face going through the baby stage again. So he chose a ready-made child of sixteen!"

He is not sure if Sophie is going to laugh or cry.

CHAPTER 9

Sophie is sitting opposite Tom in the breakfast room at De Witte Lelie. He butters a roll, takes a bite and wipes his mouth with the linen napkin. He runs both hands through his hair, trying to control the fine strands. Instead of lying flat, the hair is exactly the same as it was before the attempt to make it look tidy. Does he have the slightest idea of how his wife will spend the day? He's too preoccupied to give it a thought.

After he's left for his meeting at the Corinthia Sophie pours herself another cup of coffee and takes out a map of the city. She glances at the marks she's made on it, folds it up and puts it in her bag. With her coat over her arm, she leaves the hotel and turns right along Keizerstraat. She follows the road through Jacobsmarkt to Gemeentestraat and turns right again. Five minutes later she's standing outside the Astoria Hotel in a quiet road, next to the Stads park.

Inside there's a curved reception desk with harsh lights glistening overhead. The entrance hall has imitation leather chairs in a maroon that clashes with the tan wooden legs. At the desk the receptionist is talking to a guest. Sophie walks over to the stairs and runs up the two flights to the second floor. She is alone in the corridor and no-one hears her nails tapping on the door.

He opens immediately, as if he's been standing there, waiting. She looks at him. He holds out his arms and for a moment they are both still. Sophie puts her hand on his face and then they are kissing, laughing, moving back the few steps towards the bed. He pulls her towards him, touching her lips with his mouth. She breathes in the toothpaste taste of his teeth. For minutes they don't speak. Sophie is still breathless from running up the stairs.

"Have you got the other museum catalogue?"

"Which one? I gave you the one from the Rubens House yesterday."

"The one from MoMu, the Mode Museum."

He leans over to a pile of papers on the bedside table and hands her the booklet.

"Do you think he believes you're spending the days at these museums?"

"Yes, of course he does. I've got catalogues and brochures to prove it. Now you understand why I asked you to get them for me. I couldn't exactly have them sent to my home address in London."

As if to close the conversation she opens the buttons on his shirt, pulls him towards her and brings his face close to her lips. He feels the warmth of her breath, her kiss on his eyes. He slips both his hands under her blouse and runs his fingers over lace and bare skin.

"I can't get used to this," she says.

"And you think I can?"

He gets up and walks to the window, looking down at the parked cars. She stands behind him, putting her arms round his waist. He turns round and begins to stroke her hair, running the blonde strands through his fingers. She knows what he is thinking: How did this happen? We should have stopped it."

As if he's reading her mind he says:

"One moment we're talking about spending a night together, and ....

and then ..."

"But we decided. This is the best way to do it. You get the catalogues for me; I find the hotel room for you. This way they'll never find out."

He pulls away from her and walks over to his jacket which is draped over a chair. He reaches in the pocket for a cigarette and finds there's one left in the pack. She is twisting her hair, flicking her fringe.

He reaches for an ashtray and flicks the cigarette against the side. Sophie puts her arms round his neck, strokes the hair behind his ears. She lifts her face and brushes his lips with her mouth, feeling the warmth of the smoke in his breath. They move back to the bed.

"Let's not talk about them."

He can't see but her eyes are filling with tears. She tries to smile but can't stop her lip from trembling. She stretches out on top of him and buries her face in his shoulder, breathing in the essence of his cologne. It's a faint smell of musk and cinnamon, as if he's sprayed it in the air in front of him and just passed through it briefly. Not like the heavy signature that Tom leaves behind. He lifts his arm and turns his wrist to look at his watch:

"How long do we have? When is he back?"

"About seven."

She is wondering whether to borrow a damp towel and shower here or whether to wait till she's back in her hotel. Their brief exchange has left them both miserable. She can't explain her torment. He's probably thinking that this is all a game for her; a diversion from her life with her husband.

When she first met Tom she'd found him instantly attractive: tall, slender and well dressed. She could hardly admit to herself that his appeal was precisely the contrast between well cut suits and the baggy sweaters of her student friends. What did she know? She'd read too many romantic novels and couldn't distinguish true feelings from what she so desperately wanted to experience. On their third date she'd made the mistake of blurting out that she was in love with him.

Now years later, she has learned how to conceal her emotions. She hides the intense passion she feels for this man—the one she's come to meet in a faded hotel room. Each time they are together she thinks: "I'm going to tell him today. I'm going to tell him I love him." But she doesn't speak. What could she say? He already knows she'd rather have one snatched hour with him than a week with her husband. A whole morning lying with him is more precious than the wardrobe of designer clothes.

The bed is hard with patterned easycare sheets. The sound of a vacuum cleaner drowns out their words. No-one in the corridor can pick up their whispers and moans. If the cleaners hear anyone crying out with joy they walk discreetly by and pretend they don't know where it's coming from.

They must have been there for three hours. Sophie pulls over the covers and snuggles under his arm. Just as her eyes begin to close, he slides out of bed and begins to open some paper bags at the other side of the room.

He is getting out the food. That's his job. This time he's brought a fresh loaf, some cheese and a bottle of wine. Sophie pulls up the rose patterned sheet, holding it up under her arms. He pours the wine into a tumbler from the bathroom. They're about to share the single glass when he goes over to the chair and starts to open a paper bag.

"I've brought you a present."

He pulls out something wrapped in crisp, uncrushed tissue paper. Sophie opens it and lifts out a white cotton robe. She slips her arms into the sleeves. They are too long and come down to her finger tips.

"I know you've got all those satin things. but this is just for when you're with me. After all," he smiled "there are moments when you don't want to be dressed and you can't just wear a sheet."

She is busy pulling the belt through the slots. He looks downcast, interpreting her silence as a message that the robe is the wrong size. Far from rejecting the gift she is touched by his concern. While

Tom thinks only about how to undress her, this man is aware of her reluctance to be seen naked in full sunlight.

"It's not like the stuff you have at home?"

He still wants reassurance that the white robe is not too plain. She can read his expression and takes his hand, guiding it inside the folds of cotton.

"If you must know he bought me a camisole in a lurid pink check. The bra is see-through with silvery grey flowers and it's called Malizia. I hate it."

They finish the food. He slips the robe off her shoulders and goes over to the door.

"Where are you going?"

"Just checking. I want to make sure the sign is still there."

Outside the cleaners pass by the notice "Niet Storen—Don't disturb."

*

A light rain is falling as Sophie makes her way back to De Witte Lelie Hotel. She runs up the staircase to their room on the first floor and pulls out her suitcase. She takes out a black jersey dress, unwraps it and from the folds lifts out a bag with the name 'Ann Demeulemeester'. Inside is a white canvas jacket with straps. She crumples up the bill—'Harrods, London'. She lays the jacket out on the bed.

When Tom comes in Sophie is again coming out of the shower.

"I got soaked in the rain." she says, She hugs him and shows him the booklet from the Fashion Museum.

"Close your eyes and I'll show you what I bought."

Tom reads from the first page:

"Poetically hard-edged designs. A rich blend of tough femininity."

Sophie is wearing the canvas jacket—she turns round so he can see the back and asks him what he thinks.

"Don't ask me. It looks like a straight-jacket to me—those big straps in front, the zip and the long sleeves. When on earth are you going to wear it?"

"You don't get it, do you? This isn't just any high street jacket. Time Magazine says 'Ann Demeuelemeester has real authenticity.'"

"As opposed to producing imitation fakes?"

"You're doing it again. Picking me up on words. You know what I'm trying to say. It's all about simplicity. I'll tell you what she says: 'I wrap women in the same way as I'd wrap a table.'"

"So you might as well go out wearing a tablecloth?"

"Tom, you're being ridiculous."

She is irritated with him, for not understanding the finer points of Flemish fashion, but more for laughing at her. He makes her feel, once again, like a middle child: not as clever as her older sister, not as cute as the baby.

Tom is changing into another jacket and pulling out the cuffs of his striped shirt. As he leans over her she takes in a breath of expensive aftershave.

"Baby, I'm sorry I have to go out again. Do you want to come?"

"No, I'd rather not. You're only going to talk business. I don't mind having dinner on my own."

Sophie takes off the canvas jacket, puts on black trousers and a loose top and climbs on to the bed. She picks up the Room Service menu and glances through the salad section. After Tom has gone, she phones down to order a salade niçoise, wondering whether to add a portion of chips. Then she goes to the cupboard, takes out the white robe and puts it on the pillow, rubbing her face against the smooth cotton, trying to breathe in the smell of her lover. A knock on the door makes her jump. She folds in the sleeves, pushes the robe back in the bag and makes a space for the food on the table.

*

Barely a month after the trip to Antwerp, Sophie is packing again: this time for a trip to Italy. This is only the second time she has deceived Tom and she's going over convoluted plans to convince him that she's spending her days alone, visiting museums or shopping.

She is calm about collecting the necessary museum catalogues but it's the clothes that are giving her some concern. The purchase of a couture outfit is no simple matter. First there is the research, selecting what is up to date and different. Designs that appear in the twice yearly catwalks have to be tracked down to exclusive boutiques. Sophie can't remember when she last set foot in a department store. Quite apart from the sameness of the clothes, there are few assistants on the shop floor; certainly no-one who will engage in conversation, or show interest in matching the occasion to the perfect dress or coat.

When Sophie walks into a Bond Street emporium, she is escaping into a fantasy world, where she can forget about her real life. The feelings of loneliness and isolation disappear when the vendeuse approaches, beginning the hour-long interaction that will end in one expensive purchase. The assistant will bring out endless dresses. With each one Sophie will be reassured that her figure is just perfect, as the pounds seem to slip away. When the final choice is made and the garment is nestling in a bed of tissue paper, she waits for it to be packed in the stylish bag displaying the designer's logo. Then she makes her way to the accessories counter, where she stops to make one more purchase: a gift for Tom, or one of her sisters. For some reason she can't quite understand, this little act of generosity (albeit with Tom's money) makes her feel good, with any doubts vanishing in the perfumed air as she passes through the heavy doors to the street outside. As she leaves the glass and mirrored palace, she walks out into the sunshine with her head held high.

Back in the flat, the balloon is already beginning to deflate. If Sophie notices the price tag at all, it is only to console herself with the knowledge that having such an exclusive garment will improve her status. It will excite some envy in her dinner-party friends, contributing to the aura of cool elegance she is trying to achieve.

For her, it's of no consequence if she wears it only once, but the moment of pleasure it brings will be paid for by the inevitable discussion with Tom.

Chapter 10

In Kennington, Carla is sitting on the bed watching Joseph pack. He's filling a travel bag with clothes, completing the task in ten minutes; shirts, underwear and two pairs of silk socks (remembering that it's likely to be hot in Italy). He can feel a silent accusation, knowing that she wants to go with him.

"It's hardly worth it you coming" he tells her. "I'm only in Bologna for two days."

"So we could go together and I go on to see my parents in Arezzo."

"And how would you get back? I know you're nervous about travelling alone."

"You could come for me."

"I can't. Not if you want to stay on for a time. I have to be back in London. I've got another concert here next week."

Carla is fiddling with her hair, pulling it back behind her ears. Joseph closes his bag and zips up the conversation at the same time. There's no point suggesting she could fly back on her own. For Carla the hubbub of an airport is as fearful as Dante's inferno, only made tolerable by someone to hold her hand, hang on to her passport and find the right boarding gate.

Joseph continues: "I have an idea. Why don't you come with me another time? Perhaps I'll get a booking in Florence. That's much nearer to Arezzo. And I'll try to arrange a longer stay, so we can come back together."

Carla agrees without much argument. She has no choice. The idea of flying back alone makes her hands tremble. She can imagine standing in front of a flashing destination board, with no sign of a flight to London. The actual flight doesn't feature in her bad dream, only the arrival back at Heathrow, with an agonising wait by the luggage carousel. She can't take her eye off the belt, but at the same time she's wondering if anyone will help her with a case that's too heavy for her to lift. She floats in and out of the dream. She is gripping the empty trolley with clammy hands. As the baggage trundles round, she doesn't know which is worse: watching her case go past as she tries to grab the handle, or waiting with her eyes glazed as everyone else walks away, leaving her alone.

Joseph has found a cheap flight to Bologna from Gatwick airport. He slumps into the train, relieved that his discussion with Carla was shorter than he'd expected. By the time he's on the plane he's beginning to look forward to his two days away. The aircraft touches down at G. Marconi airport. Joseph takes the bus from outside the terminal and fumbles in his pocket for the pack of euros he needs for the fare. The journey to the centre of the city takes twenty minutes and his hotel, the Pedrini, is a short walk from the bus. He humps his overnight bag on to his shoulder, walks past the piazza and finds the entrance. He registers at the desk, notices that there's a café next door to have breakfast and goes up to room Fourteen. It's small and overheated, as if they still have the central heating on. If it's this warm in May, he can't imagine what it's like in high summer, with no air-conditioning and the overhead fan clicking and whirring through the night.

He must have been waiting for three hours. The ashtray is full. He paces back and forth to the window, looks out, and forces himself to sit down at the desk. His right leg is vibrating. Finally she arrives.

"Darling, I'm so sorry. I'll explain later."

He holds her with both arms, almost squeezing the breath out of her. He doesn't tell her how long he's been there, unable to settle to anything, waiting for her to come.

Sophie closes her eyes, feeling the warmth of him, the faint bristles on his chin, then draws away. She pulls a folder from her bag and hands him a printed sheet. Without looking at it Joseph asks:

"So, where am I supposed to be playing?"

"The Teatro Comunale di Bologna."

"O Dio, ma no."

"Joseph, what's wrong?"

"That's the opera house. I know I'm successful, but that's ridiculous. It's much more likely to be the Accademia."

"Where's that?"

"The Accademia Filarmonica. If you're going to write the reviews of my performances, you've got to get the place right."

"I'm not sure about doing the reviews."

"Tesoro, we agreed. You write something about my performance; I show it to Carla and if she sees it in black and white it'll never cross her mind that I didn't go to do a concert."

"So tell me, how do I go about writing them? I'm not a journalist and I don't know anything about music either."

"It's easy. You get it from people who do know. When we get back I'll show you some of the real reviews I've had. What you can do is look on the internet. You're good at that, aren't you? You just copy bits of reviews of famous pianists and put in my name instead of, say, Maurizio Pollini."

"How do you spell that?" Sophie takes out a piece of paper and starts to make notes.

"Ma-u-r-i-zio. Try Murray Perahia or Brendel, his first name's easier, it's Alfred."

She scrunches up the piece of paper, takes out another one and writes the initials MP, MP and AB.

"That's enough to remind me."

She is slipping off her shoes. She goes to lie down on the bed.

"... and, the shopping—where am I ... ?

"Don't talk."

He puts his hand behind her back and begins to peel down the zip on her dress. He kisses her lips, opening his mouth.

"No, just a minute, let's go over where I'm supposed to be shopping. You told me to bring La Perla underwear."

Joseph vaguely remembers a discussion about what Sophie could buy in London that would be available in Bologna. She is still talking:

"It's back at the hotel. I took it out of the bag so he'll never know I bought it in Sloane Street."

"So you'll tell him you got it here?"

"Darling, on this I've done my homework properly. There's a La Perla boutique in ... where is it? Galleria Cavour. I never had any idea that the company started from a tiny workshop here in Bologna. Did you know?"

"Me? No, I don't know anything about fashion."

He doesn't tell her that Carla used to buy handmade lace and embroidery with a label 'La Perla Bologna'.

"Forget about the underwear."

He is unclipping a hook and stroking the skin under the straps of her soft triangular bra. The edgy mood has given way to a distracted look. She knows immediately what he is thinking. It's not the first time that their hours together are overlaid with unspoken thoughts of guilt and concern.

"Joseph?"

"Hmm?"

"You're not entirely here, are you?"

He moves away. Runs his fingers through his hair. Takes out a cigarette.

"Of course I'm not. What am I doing Sophie?"

"You're spending two days—not even two whole days—away from all the pressure, the worry about how Carla is feeling."

"Yes, but if she knew, just imagine."

"That's why it's a secret. Why neither of them must ever find out. How is it hurting them if their lives carry on the same?"

"That's just the point; their lives are the same, but we ... we're living in two worlds. It's not just the places, like you and me together in these different cities, It's slipping from one life into another and all the time, the bad feelings."

"Joseph, you have to put her out of your mind. Forget about it. Just for a few days."

"I want to."

He's stroking the hair that's blonde—not black; feeling the manicured nails that are long and square cut. His lips brush the pale eyelashes, darkened with expensive mascara. His tongue moves down her fair skin, feeling the length of her body. A memory of Carla bursts into his head. The honeymoon. A small hotel by the sea. On the beach he's oiling her back and watching as her body turns nut brown. At night he laughs as she takes off her bikini and shows him the triangles of white skin.

"Help me Sophie. Help me."

She lifts her legs and squeezes him closer. He can hear her whispering "Joseph, my love." It's a long time since he's heard words like that. She says it again. "My love."

*

He's been married to Carla for eight years; she was barely out of her teens when the piano playing first threatened to take him away from her. He'd won a place to study at the Conservatory in Perugia. It was only two stations from Arezzo on the train, but it seemed to them both as far away as Vienna. Carla's world revolved around 'casa' and 'piazza'. At home her job was to help her mother—going out to work wasn't an option. After dark the girls in the town spilled out of their homes, dressed in clothes that were neatly pressed, spending the hours after dinner walking arm in arm, eyeing the boys as they revved their motorbikes. In those languid summer evenings life seemed easy with no problems beyond the choice of a suitable mate.

Joseph knew that his future lay outside Italy and set about convincing Carla to go with him to London. Their furtive fumblings had convinced her that he would make a fine husband and lover, so partly, it must be said, to annoy her parents, she agreed to the move.

After they married—a wedding day Joseph preferred to forget—they began a life away from family, friends and the whole community they'd grown up with. Joseph had to earn a living. Carla was alone in a strange country with fiendish weather and a language with impossible spelling and pronunciation.

To help with her English, Joseph suggested they should go to films. Carla's taste was for romantic movies: Ghost or Pretty Woman. Joseph would have preferred action films, but even at the cinema he found himself playing music in his head, moving his fingers to remember difficult passages. Carla would slap his hand and then cuddle up to him in the dark. But if he whispered words of love to her, she would be embarrassed and tell him to keep his eyes on the film.

*

The heat in the room is intense. When they wake up, Sophie's hair is damp. Joseph goes over to the window, which is stuck fast. He bangs at the wooden frame and then gives up.

"It's unbearable in here. Let's go out."

"Where to?" she asks.

"If you feel like climbing five hundred steps we could go up one of the famous towers. Or we could go to Chiesa di S. Bartolomeo. On third thoughts, it might be better if we go to a park. We're less likely to collide with him."

"Joseph, you're so funny."

"What did I say?"

"You don't collide with someone, you bump into them."

"Well, we're less likely to bump him if we go to that park. It's called Cassini, or Cassarini, non lo so. It's supposed to have pomegranate trees."

"Joseph. Stop talking about parks and trees and come here."

The way he kisses her is studied, careful—almost in slow motion. For twenty minutes he explores the map of her body, finding inlets and peaks, moving his hand as she discovers the pleasure of a touch on an ear, inside an elbow.

"Jo ... where did you learn.?"

"Learn what?"

"How to make love like this?"

Her voice drops and she bites her lip. She can't stop herself from blurting out: "Have you had lots of women?"

He laughs and winds his arms round her.

"You won't believe it, but Carla was the first. I knew her since we were children."

A look of sadness comes over Sophie's face.

"So, what do you want me to say? That I've had a hundred lovers?"

"I don't know what I want you to say. The trouble is that I don't want you to have a past."

She was going to add "and I can't see any future for us" when he replied:

"Sophie, we're so good at it. Making each other feel guilty."

"I didn't mean to. I expect if we'd done this before we'd be used to it—the deception, the collusion. But we have so little time, so let's not talk about it any more."

He doesn't comment. He is waiting for her to make the first move, embarrassed at her comments about the practised way he makes love. The truth is not exactly what he's told Sophie. Carla was his first girlfriend but not his first lover. When he was sixteen his father had given him the most extraordinary of birthday presents. He'd handed him three envelopes, each containing several notes. When Joseph asked what the money was for, his father replied "for you to learn about life." The next day he took him to a part of Arezzo that he'd never been to before. They arrived at an old building and walked up some stairs to a room on the second floor. The door was opened by a woman in her thirties, wearing a wrap over dress of a silky material that didn't quite cover her breasts. She smiled at them. Joseph was wondering how to deal with the money when he realised his father had gone and they were alone.

Sophie is looking at him with liquid eyes, He may have been taught techniques for pleasing women but at this moment all he can do is wait. He is willing her to say the words again—the two words 'my love'. He wants to hear her say that wherever he is, he is at the centre of all her waking thoughts. Eventually he breaks the silence.

"When do you have to be back?"

"Six. I don't want him to be there before me."

CHAPTER 11

The Grand Hotel Baglioni in Bologna has a restaurant with 16th century frescoes on the ceiling. A red carpeted staircase with a wrought-iron balustrade leads to the first floor. Tom has reserved a suite with white columns and a bed swathed in soft voile curtains.

At ten o'clock Sophie crosses the marbled hall with its tinkling chandelier and walks out into Via dell'Indipendenza. The meaning of the name isn't lost on her. She crosses the piazza passing under the porticos and arrives at the Pedrini Hotel, out of breath. She knocks on the door of room Fourteen.

"I know I'm early. It's to make up for yesterday. I never got a chance to explain why I kept you waiting so long. He's done a deal with a chain of hotels called Star. There's one near the station with nearly 200 rooms. He wanted me to see it. God knows why. He never asks my opinion on what to put on the walls, but for some reason he insisted that I go with him."

"You don't think he's assumed something?"

Joseph's English is getting worse. As he's in Bologna he is thinking in Italian. The conversation that comes out of his mouth is a muddle of English and phrases from his native language.

Sophie pulls the cotton robe out of a bag and begins to unbutton his shirt:

"Of course he doesn't know. He said I looked tired yesterday. I told him it was walking up all those towers."

"I was thinking of you last night—having dinner, eating ... what did you order? I hope you didn't ask for spaghetti Bolognese."

"Joseph, give me some credit. But we did start with some kind of pasta with a meat sauce, then we had calamari." She runs her finger over the smooth skin on his chest.

"I wish you and I could have dinner together."

"It's impossible." He pulls her hand away. "Sophie, don't do that."

"What's the matter? Don't you want to?"

"Yes, but not now. Let's go down and have a coffee."

Joseph walks over to the basin and splashes his face with cold water.

"This heat, it's giving me a headache."

"Do you think it's sensible? To go to the cafe? We might be seen."

"Sophie, cara, we can't stay in here all day."

They go into the bar. She finds a table in the corner and Joseph brings over an espresso and a cappuccino.

They both speak at once: Sophie says:

"I thought it better not to sit outside."

He is still standing: "Do you want something to eat? a bombolone?"

"Yes, I want three, because I love them. All that creamy filling inside and the sugar on top. But I'm not going to."

"Why not? I'd like to see you eat one."

"Because. it's the one thing I'm strong minded about, not eating cakes. It's habit. I suppose I just accept all that pressure on women to be slim. As long as I can remember I've been told that eating sweet things is a sin."

"I can think of a worse one." Joseph smiles and throws back his espresso in one gulp.

"I suppose it goes back to when I was young. Gemma was prettier and Debs was clever. The only thing I had going for me was that I was slim. Well not slim, skinny. They called me Daddy Long Legs, but I hated them, the way they came inside in the summer, flying around and landing on a windowsill."

"You've lost me. Whose Daddy? and who's flying around?"

"Sorry, Daddy Long Legs—it's a kind of insect. Did you know that it has four pairs of legs? If it's in danger of getting caught, it can break off a portion of one of its legs and then escape. The detached leg goes on quivering. Then later it can grow a new leg."

"You're not serious?"

"When I used to get upset, I thought I'd show them. If they hurt my feelings, I could just grow some more."

"You say such funny things."

Joseph puts his hand on her arm and moves his fingers under the silk of her sleeve.

"But they're not really funny are they? Tell me what it was like ... before you met him."

"Where do you want me to start? I've told you about when I was little. And about my sisters."

"Wait a minute. Let's get some more coffee."

He brings back two cups and a plate with the doughnut. He cuts it in half and checks to see that it has the right amount of custard inside.

"Which half do you want? OK, sorry, now you can tell me. I won't interrupt any more."

"I don't think anyone noticed me growing up. Everything that happened was somehow related to Gemma or Debs. When I was eleven, I found that I was bleeding—you know—no-one had told me, so I tried to look in a mirror, to see where it was coming from. I knew I hadn't cut myself and I was more mystified than worried. Anyway, the next day, it hadn't stopped and it was coming more and more. So I put on two pairs of pants and in the evening I tried to wash out the blood. My mother must have found the wet pants, but even then she didn't explain it to me. You probably think it was extraordinary that I didn't know—what with having an older sister, but we were so ... so separate."

"So you were ... how you say, finally a woman?"

Joseph is thinking that at that age he was still a boy. Sophie sees a look of sadness cross his face.

"Tell me," she says softly.

"It's nothing. It's that I had a passion when I was eleven. I could only think of one thing—football. I was chosen to play for the school. Then for the town. We went to a big competition, in Portugal, but it was not good."

"What do you mean?" Sophie is wiping the sugar from her mouth.

"When we went out to play all the spectators started to hiss and then they began to shout 'Port-u-gal, Port-u-gal'. Near the end of the game—we were one down—there was a penalty kick and I was chosen to do it. Everyone was waiting. I ran up, I kicked the ball and it hit the top of the goal post. I'd lost the match. I never forget it. There was such a silence and then the other team, they started shouting 'Ar-e-zzo, pazzo, Ar-ezzo, pazzo.'"

"What does pazzo mean?"

"It means crazy. I think it also means what we are doing."

For a few minutes they sit looking at the empty coffee cups. Joseph breaks the silence:

"You're supposed to be telling me about your life."

Sophie doesn't know where to begin. He won't be interested in how she got a place to read History of Art at Southampton University. She wonders whether to tell him about her mother? She is thinking about that first term. It was the September when her mother told her she had breast cancer. Sophie was going to lectures and her friends were deciding which clubs to join: Roller Hockey, Hang-gliding, Chamber Choir. But all she could think about was her mother undergoing radiotherapy. When she came home for Christmas everyone assured her that the cancer was under control. At the end of the vacation she was getting ready to go back to

Southampton when she had a huge row with her father. She begins to tell Joseph about it.

"I was packing up to go back to university. I had all these books and too many boxes and my father said I'd never get them all on the train. And then we started arguing and he said: 'Why did you have to go to a university at the other end of the country?' And I said: 'Because none of you seem to mind much where I am.' And then Mum, she tried to calm us down and I went to the station and that was the last time I saw her."

Joseph doesn't say a word. He moves his chair nearer to Sophie and strokes her face.

His finger is wet and he puts it in his mouth, licking her tears.

"Hey, what am I doing telling you all this? It's fine now. I get on much better with them. Debs has gone to work in New York and Gemma's married with three children."

Sophie stops before adding: "She doesn't have much of a life. How could she with three little ones?"

"Didn't you ever want children?" Joseph is drinking his second espresso and lights up a cigarette.

"No. It seems so hard. I've stayed there and heard the crying. It goes on and on. Even when you get up and feed the baby, half an hour later it starts again. If it's not the baby, it's the three year old, crying because she's had a bad dream. Either way, you get no sleep, you wake up and stagger out of bed, change the nappies."

"Sophie, they grow up. It's not all negative."

"That's how it seems to me. Gemma looks so drawn, she can't even go to the loo on her own without a little person knocking on the door."

Joseph looks bewildered:

"But little children, they're so beautiful, their perfect skin, their big eyes, the white of the sclera."

"What's that?"

"You know, the part ... the part of the eye. See, with an older person, it doesn't have that look, like a pearl. It goes yellow."

Sophie smiles.

"So it makes it better to look at their eyes while you're changing the nappies?"

Joseph goes on as if he's not listening to her.

"You know, little children, how they trust you, how they think you know everything. My nephew, Aldo, he once squeezed out a whole tube of toothpaste on the floor. He was about three. My brother came in and looked down at the mess—a long ribbon of white, all sticky. Aldo looked up at him with big sad eyes and said 'Papa, put it back.'"

"So how come you and Carla don't have children, if you like them so much?"

"It's a long story. When we met, in Arezzo, I was still at school. In the evenings all the boys would walk round the town together, looking at the girls. I was always watching Carla and one day she looked back at me. We went together from that day. So we decide to get married. Her parents, they didn't want it, They didn't like me because I want to take their daughter away. They call me 'the monster'. Why you want to go with that monster? Why you not stay here?"

Sophie is laughing and puts her hand up to her mouth.

"So anyway, we get married. Her mother, she makes a big party. All the neighbours, for days they are cooking and they make a long table. After the church, all the day, her father—he doesn't say one word to me. Then they bring on the cake. It's made with crema and butter and espresso and rum and roasted almonds—oh, it's amazing. So we are cutting the cake and he is standing next to me and he says: 'Don't forget. She is only on loan to you. She's mine and she can come back when she wants.'"

"What happened next, after the monster took her away? Were you happy when you first came to England?"

"Yes, for a while. We come to London, we find a flat and I am travelling. I go to play in competitions, in church halls, and I win a prize. At a Festival in York. I get an engagement with a local symphony orchestra. So I am away from home and Carla is sad. She doesn't speak good English—worse than me."

He smiles, runs his finger around Sophie's wrist and along the white skin of her arm.

"So why didn't you stay in London?"

"I found an agent, Richard Adams. He finds the work. I go where the work is. And Carla, she gets depressed. She begins to think she is ill. But I know these pains she has, in her chest, in her arm, she imagines it. She is—what you call it—ipocondriaca. Every time I go away, she tells me she is in pain, but the pain gets better when I walk in the door."

"Do you have rows when you get back?"

"No, she is ... she is silent. She doesn't talk much. She cooks, we eat and I play piano. She doesn't like when I practise, when I go over and over a piece, it makes her cross. She doesn't like it. Eh, what can I do? I play five hours in a day."

Sophie's coffee is getting cold. She takes his hand and they go back up to his room.

Joseph begins to take off her clothes, gently, laying each item on the floor by the side of the bed. Weeks before, Sophie might have been embarrassed by the size of her thighs or the thread veins at the back of her leg. Now she can laugh at her less-than-perfect body.

"Tom says I'm pear-shaped" says Sophie as Joseph runs his lips over her stomach.

"He says a lot of things I don't agree with. He doesn't understand you at all. And he doesn't know what makes you happy."

They are interrupted by the phone. Sophie leans over to pick up the receiver. Joseph puts his fingers on her mouth and shakes his head as he takes the call.

"Pronto. Si Carla, domani, certo." Joseph lights a cigarette and lets out a long breath. "She wants to know when I'm coming home."

CHAPTER 12

After the Paris trip, Tom decides that Sophie should always go with him when he has business in Europe. He books them into a first-class hotel and while he is working Sophie is out all day shopping or going to museums. Being on her own never seems to worry her. In the evenings they go over the catalogues together, looking at details of brushstrokes and shadow.

It's strange. In London, there is no mention of galleries. How does Sophie spend her time? Friends from university never feature in her conversation so heaven knows what she does all day. There's a black desk in the spare room with a computer that they share. The printer is underneath the chrome legs, out of sight. His side of the desk is usually tidy with a file that says 'My Move' and another with the words 'Your Move'—a variation on an 'in' and 'out' tray. Her section has scribbled notes and a sheet headed 'Passwords'. How could she leave them in full view, when the whole point of a password is to keep it secret? She seems to like surfing the internet—probably searching for more clothes. Apparently you can watch a video of the latest designs on the catwalk. She prints out pictures from the collections; dresses and suits she will never wear. Sometimes her notes spread over to his side. He finds one with the letters MP, MP and AB. He can't work it out—Missoni, Moschino, Burberry?

Their interests are so different. Sophie seems happy with her own company and is even reluctant to go out. He comes back from a day negotiating with artists and hotel owners and when he tells her about it, a far away look comes into her eyes, as if she isn't listening to what he's saying.

But when they are away, it's all different. Sophie comes to life, full of energy and enthusiasm for seeing new places. In the evenings she is usually back in the room before he returns. As Tom slides the key into the door he knows what to expect. There will be a pile of new clothes laid out on the bed and often something else: a small package, wrapped and ribboned. This is a present for him: a pair of travel speakers for his personal stereo or a zinc corkscrew. Once it was a fine Japanese knife. The gifts are always bought in London, never from the city they're in. It's as if Sophie wants to choose something for him before she goes shopping for herself. But judging from Sophie's mood, buying clothes must be as exhausting as spending the day in negotiation. By the time they meet up in the evenings neither of them has much energy for anything more than dinner and bed.

Back in London their life is different. They go to the theatre and dinner parties. Tom likes to go out, keeping up a constant chatter about his travels and the work he is commissioning. But these outings are a source of friction between them. An hour before they leave the flat, Sophie stands at her wardrobe, flicking through the hangers. She pulls out trousers and jackets, holding them up in front of a mirror. After half an hour there are fifteen discarded outfits on the bed. She finally makes a choice. Her current favourite is Moschino; an A-line wool skirt with black stitching and a corsage belt. It cost £885. The wool felt coat she wears on top has oversize buttons and is from the Moschino Cheap & Chic range. It only cost £760. He knows all this because she tells him, as she dresses slowly and invariably makes them late.

At the dinner party the host offers a glass of wine or gin and tonic. There are usually eight or ten guests and the conversation centres on work or children. Sophie is uncomfortable talking about either of these topics. She slides to the edge of her chair as a five-year old totters over with a dish of salted nuts in one hand and oily black olives in the other. She sits listening, replying to questions with a forced smile. At dinner she is seated between two men and tries to steer the discussion to places she's been to with Tom. She seems to know a lot about the towers in Bologna and the diamond business in Antwerp. Across the table she picks up snippets of conversation 'beautiful child, or she will be when her braces come off', 'that marvellous new florist where they make up bouquets scented with truffle oil'.

When the food is passed round Sophie never seems to be hungry, pushing the grilled sea bass to the edge of her plate, toying with the avocado and chilli salsa on the side. She welcomes the salad course, helping herself to rocket and oak leaf lettuce. The men are refilling the wine glasses. The hostess makes a space on the table for the desserts. Tom is too busy talking to notice what's on his plate. All the women ask for 'just a tiny bit', picking up the smaller of the two spoons to dip into the crème brûlée or melting chocolate pudding. None of them would dream of having a second helping. At midnight the host offers to bring the coats. 'Is yours the sheepskin or the suede?' The guests exchange kisses on the doorstep and each couple walks down the path to their car, exchanging brief words about the amount of wine they've consumed. The one who has drunk the least aims the remote at the lock and settles into the driver's seat. When they get back to the flat Sophie looks drained. She is waiting for Tom's inevitable comment:

"We have to reciprocate. That's the second time we've been there."

She hangs up her clothes in the cupboard, placing each item on a separate padded hanger and wrapping it in it's plastic cover.

"It takes days to make a dinner like that. Can you see me turning out a layered terrine or whisking up a pavlova roulade?"

"Well."

Sophie doesn't wait for his reply.

"And then there's the table decorations. I think one of them went on a course to learn how to do it—bowls of pebbles set on huge mirrors, black tablecloths with shimmering twigs."

Tom looks at his watch. He doesn't want to press her on returning the hospitality.

"I rather liked those flower arrangements at each place setting. What was it—rose buds wrapped in banana leaves?"

Sophie is silent, not sure if he's being serious. She looks around their own living-room where there's not a newspaper or magazine on show; no sticky fingerprints on the glass table.

What is she thinking? Tom sighs and considers a suggestion.

"Why don't we take them out for dinner?"

"Why not? Wherever we are the conversation will be the same. They'll talk about the problems with nannies: 'Do you know you even have to provide an iPod now, so they can listen to music while they wait in the 4 x 4 outside school. You should have seen little Ludo. He was the third shepherd, though of course they don't call it a nativity play any more. It's the holiday play. It's so important for them to know about Chanucah and Diwali, don't you think?"

"What would you like to talk about, Sophie?" Tom sounds exasperated.

"Let's forget it. Come to bed."

Tom has to be up early in the morning. They get undressed, brush their teeth and make love. The whole bedtime ritual takes no longer than fifteen minutes.

CHAPTER 13

Richard Adams is Joseph's agent. He had started in business at an early age. When he was thirteen he discovered the possibilities of buying and selling in the school lunch break. Whatever was the current craze, the object of the moment, he would know where to obtain it. How he knew this was not clear to his fellow students. In fact he was often the one to create the craze. He'd buy a quantity of a cheap electronic gadget and offer the item to a few friends at a 'special price'. When the news spread, he let it be known that he might just be able to lay his hands on a few more. Most of the boys thought he was doing them a favour in obtaining them. Hardly any of them realised that the gadgets were being sold at a profit.

In the sixth form he became a prefect. During lessons he resented being told what to do by the teachers. In the playground he could wield power over the younger boys in ways that were not obvious; he would send a ten-year-old to clear up the changing room, or start a quarrel by demanding that four footballs were brought to him in the next five minutes. The younger children regarded him with a mixture of fear and admiration. By the time he left school it was clear that he was no scholar. He had other talents: organising poker games and working on the lighting for theatre productions. At university he spent his time in the bar, helping students negotiate a change of accommodation or recruiting actors for plays. It was no surprise that he got a mediocre degree. He left with what was commonly known as a 'Desmond' (a Tutu, or 2.2).

In his twenties he drifted in and out of jobs until he discovered that he was best at organising other people. It didn't matter that he couldn't do something himself; he would find someone who could. So he became a talent scout, enjoying the power of selecting and rejecting performers. Once a contract for a gig or concert was signed, he merely needed to make a few follow-up phone calls for regular amounts of money to fall into his account.

*

Although he has a couple of classical musicians on his books, Richard knows nothing about the concert world. As literary agents probably have no idea about the structure of sentences, the endless thought that goes into cutting, re-writing and perfecting a novel, so Richard has no conception of the work involved in bringing a page of sheet music to life, translating the thoughts of the composer into a flawless performance.

He has developed the habit of 'dropping in' on his clients 'just to see how they are getting on'. He would never have the time for such visits if he had a stable of pianists and violinists, all clamouring for his promotion. When he arrives at Braganza Street, Joseph is working on a Chopin Concerto.

"Why are you playing a piece that needs an orchestra? I don't have the London Philharmonic lined up for you."

Joseph sees no point in responding and lets Richard continue:

"Surely you'd do better to practise the pieces in your programme?"

Joseph has no wish to explain the way he works; to elaborate on the beauty and passion behind a piece of Chopin. He restricts his reply to talking about the technical challenge:

"If I can play Chopin, I can play almost anything."

He moves to a passage dominated by thirds. Even Richard can hear the gentle lyricism. Joseph doesn't bother to tell him that the orchestral part is almost superfluous. It isn't like Beethoven where there's a dialogue between the orchestra and the soloist. He has chosen this piece because he's thinking of Sophie when he is practising. It's a huge aria for piano, breathlessly melodic, with flashing trills that need a light touch, a loose hand.

Richard has wandered into the kitchen. The first movement seems to be slowing down, but then instead of lifting his fingers off the notes, Joseph continues into the dazzling climax before the pianist would hand over to the orchestra. Carla is out shopping so Richard makes himself a cup of tea and brings it over to the piano where he wants to continue the conversation. He tries a question:

"Did Chopin compose this when he was old?"

"No. He never was old. He died at thirty-nine. Actually he wrote this when he was nineteen and in love with a beautiful student. She married someone else."

Joseph is thinking that Richard can have no idea of the turmoil in his own life; the secret assignations with Sophie, the guilt-ridden trips abroad. For the hundredth time he goes back to the chance meeting that started a whirlwind sweeping through his mind and his work—tearing away at the marriage he thought was stable.

CHAPTER 14

They met in a park. It was Carla's complaint that made him rush out of the flat in a fury. Joseph had been practising a short piece, playing it again and again. His wife had broken his concentration, protesting, as usual, about the repetition. He could handle her depression, even summoning up sympathy for the black moods that lasted from morning till night. But when her negative thoughts had an impact on his work, he lost patience and thought only of how he was struggling to earn a living in a competitive world.

He remembers that it was a Prokofiev Etude that sparked off the conversation that led to his fit of temper.

"It doesn't even have a tune, this piece" says Carla.

"That's not the point of it. An étude is designed to help with technique. It's meant as practice material."

"But you are going over and over the same notes."

"That's because I'm trying to get it right. I'm trying not to watch what my left hand is doing. I have to hit the correct base note without taking my eyes off what's happening with my right hand. These pieces are difficult. It's about how the fingers work."

"I don't think Chopin lived in a tiny apartment, annoying everyone around him."

"It's not Chopin. It's Prokofiev."

"Whichever one. I like the longer pieces better. You don't stop so much."

"That's precisely the point. This piece only lasts for two minutes. There are hundreds of notes to remember."

"Was there a Mrs. Prokofiev?"

Joseph doesn't answer and hurls the music on to the ground. He rushes out of the flat without closing the door. He walks down Braganza Street, jumping on to the first bus that comes along. He is shaking as he realizes he's forgotten to bring a coat or even a sweater. At Westminster he gets off the bus and walks into St. James' Park.

By this time it's starting to rain and it's drizzling on his hair and shirt. At first the rain is light, but then the sky darkens and the drops seem more persistent. He looks for somewhere to shelter and sits down on a park bench under a tree. Next to him is a young woman. She has straight blonde hair and is wearing gloves. He sneaks another look at her. She has flawless skin, almost white, and the arc of each eyebrow seems to be slightly different. She is wearing a long coat but he can see from the way it hangs that underneath she has a slender build. They start up a conversation about the weather. Minutes later, they are sitting at a table, drinking cappuccinos in a cafe. He begins to tell her about his work and before he realises it, his coffee has got cold and he has told her about his quarrel with Carla.

"I'm sorry. I don't know why I'm telling you all this."

"Because you can't tell your wife you're angry with her."

"And I can tell you?"

She's looking straight at him and he looks back at her grey eyes and pale skin. He's trying to work out what makes her face so perfect. Perhaps it's the arrangement of the eyebrows, the width between the eyes, the slight curve of the mouth.

The young woman runs her fingers through her hair and shakes out what looks like an expensive silk scarf.

"Aren't you cold? You don't have a jacket."

"No, I'm fine."

"So tell me about the concert."

"It's just a lunchtime concert."

"What are you going to play?"

"Some modern things, Prokofiev Etudes, something by Siegmeister and a Mozart piece. That's the one I'm worried about. I've never played it in public before."

She doesn't say anything trite like 'well, there has to be a first time.' Instead she asks him to tell her about the composer she's never heard of. Joseph is enjoying his explanation.

"In a way, it's easier if the programme is well known. You don't have to sell the work when you're looking for a venue—just yourself."

"Does that mean you choose Mozart more often?"

"I choose him because of the shape of my hands."

"What do you mean?"

"Every pianist has different hands—the shape, the size, the muscularity. If your hands are like Chopin's you'll play his work better, follow the instinctive movement of how he played. If you've got massive hands, like John Ogden, say, they're too big for Mozart. The gentle passages need finesse."

By now the rain has stopped and they say goodbye, awkwardly. He has no recollection of it, but he must have told her the date of the concert and that it would be at St. Martin-in-the-Fields.

*

He walks on to the stage, sits down and adjusts the piano stool. This is the moment of pure hell. He reminds himself that any performer who says he's not nervous is either a liar, or has a short memory. He turns to look up. That's when he notices that she is there, in the fourth row. The C Major sonata begins with the allegro that he's been trying to perfect. He plays it with a light-fingered sparkle and by the time he rolls into the andante he is playing with no effort, closing his eyes and relaxing into the pensive mood. After each movement when he would normally take his eyes off the keys, he makes sure he doesn't look in her direction. He stops briefly after the Mozart and continues with the rest of the programme. At the end of the performance, the audience is appreciative. Joseph feels he's got the touch right and achieved an evenness in the arpeggio passages, but as ever he wonders how good it was. Usually he stays to chat with the few enthusiasts waiting to talk to him but this time he leaves the building without hanging around and sees her walking down the steps into the drizzle of Trafalgar Square. He goes up behind her, puts his hand on her elbow and says:

"There aren't any trees here, but since it's raining again, would you like a coffee?"

She turns and smiles, with a slow lifting of her eyes. In the cafe Joseph starts to talk about the Mozart:

"It's not often performed, the K279. I didn't get the tempo right in the last movement."

"It all sounded brilliant to me".

"Eh, forse. It might ... if you've never heard Mitsuko playing."

"I'm afraid I haven't. Should I know about him?"

"It's not a him, it's a her: Mitsuko Uchida."

"Right."

Neither of them speaks for a moment. Maybe she's never heard of the Japanese pianist. Only a musician would know that Uchida is the most technically perfect of all Mozart performers. As if she has read his thoughts she asks:

"Tell me what's so great about her."

"She has a lightness ... how you say? A delicacy, such a brilliant technique, with just the right amount of emotion."

"I thought you put a lot of emotion into your playing."

She looks directly at him. She is so straightforward, not embarrassed at her lack of musical knowledge.

He looks down and then says:

"Do you know, you haven't even told me your name."

"You never told me yours, but I found out, didn't I?"

"So, come on, what is it?"

"Sophie. And I'm married too."

CHAPTER 15

A few days after the concert at St. Martin-in-the Fields they are sitting in a Turkish restaurant, at an outside table, ordering mezze. Joseph is the one who has suggested lunch.

"I can't believe I'm doing this, I'm not like that."

"Like what?" she asks.

"You know—those men who look at other women. They can't wait for the summer because it gives them a chance to look at short skirts and bare legs. They are always looking at big ... you know."

He makes a gesture and then falls silent. He can't believe he is having lunch with a woman who is not his wife. He's always thought of himself as happily married, but if this is true why is he sitting opposite a beautiful woman, smiling, unable to keep his eyes off her? Perhaps the words 'happy' and 'married' don't necessarily go together. He has come to accept life as it is. It's enough that he wakes up eager to play music and goes to bed content that his hands are moving more swiftly over the notes.

After their first lunch date they meet again. Within minutes their fingers are touching across the table and when they part those same fingers are busy making contact by phone or text five times a day. They put off the inevitable. They talk about it, yet it never happens in London. It's a month before they face each other, in a foreign hotel, waking to the realisation of what they have done. Adulterio—the word is still shocking in his Catholic world. Yet what stuns him more is that Sophie has shaken him out of the illusion that his home life is satisfactory and reveals what is wrong in his relationship with Carla and her constant complaint about his practising. Sophie has given him back his confidence. Though she has little knowledge of music, she assures him that few members of the audience will notice a missed note. She buys Chinese tea to calm him down and even opens a discussion on his smoking habit.

"I wish you'd give up cigarettes."

"So does someone else."

"Who's that?" she asks, guessing that he's referring to his wife.

"The person who writes on the packets."

"What do you mean?"

"That man who writes in big letters, on every pack of cigarettes: SMOKING KILLS."

They end up laughing. The subject is closed.

*

In Sophie's marriage it is never Tom who needs encouragement or praise. She is the one who craves reassurance—about her shape, her ability to shine in a social gathering. She is wrong, of course. Her figure is only a few pounds short of perfect. Others see her as a calm, introspective beauty. Mothers of small children envy her style and assume her reticence with little people is because she is unable to have a child herself. They have no idea of her tearful conversations with Tom, explaining why they should never join the treadmill of starting a family. He retreats ever more into his world of work, emulating the perfection of soulless hotel rooms, guiding her towards taste and refinement that would be the envy of their friends in their cluttered, toy-filled spaces.

Sophie is lonely. She is loyal enough never to divulge to a friend her grievances about her husband or the fears that alienate her from the couples whose lives revolve around children. For a while the buying of designer clothes conforms to Tom's image of the perfect wife, but now he seems to have little sympathy with her acquisitions. His lack of understanding makes her want to accumulate even more outfits—clothes that lack lustre in her eyes minutes after they are removed from the bag, taking up space in finely crafted built-in furniture.

She isn't looking for an adventure, an affair. When Joseph's fingers brush her arm and he speaks of the music that fills his days, she forgets her limited life and imagines that together they can each escape from the strain of striving for perfection.

*

The deception becomes easier. They are so confident: so sure that Carla has no suspicion of what they are doing. They have everything covered. As soon as Sophie hears that she is going abroad with Tom, she buys Joseph a cheap package to the same city. She finds out about local concert halls and invents an engagement for him. Then comes the harder task of concocting a fictitious review. Joseph has shown Sophie cuttings about his real concerts so she has learned how to describe the 'clarity and deftness' of his playing, the 'point, shape and purpose' in the performance. She uses her computer to compose the review, prints it out in the form of a press release, mentioning the local paper where it has supposedly appeared. He shows Carla the one from Antwerp but has some explaining to do when the reviews of his Italian concerts appear in English. He manages to persuade Carla that all reviews are translated as you can't expect an international audience to understand European languages. Fortunately it never occurs to Carla to buy the real newspapers and she seems happy that the critics think so well of her husband. Sophie is getting good at the wording. She searches the internet for notes on CDs and interviews between critics and performers.

"Listen to this Joseph."

"Hmm?"

"His piano sat majestically alone on the stage. He was at his best when interpreting gentle tones, barely touching the keys, yet filling the hall with passion and emotional resonance."

"Who's that about, Brendel or Schiff?"

"It doesn't matter. It's about you now. But you didn't let me finish. I'm going to put in some more. Listen ..."

"The Schubert was a study in perfectly defined pastel shades. In the Mozart the scherzo was a flourish of arpeggios and the main theme of the andante was picked out in haunted relief."

It's hard enough for Joseph to confront the guilt he feels at betraying Carla. When it overlaps with his work it unsettles him. He finds himself repeating those complimentary phrases as he plays. Added to the high standards he's already set himself, the burden of attaining perfection makes his fingers so tight that sometimes he can't even hit the right notes.

Joseph prefers it when they are discussing the museum catalogues. Sophie arranges to have them sent to Kennington, as they both assume that Carla will never open his post. She'll think that the thick envelopes contain information on the cities where he is performing and she'll have no idea that they are part of a complicated alibi. Carla comes from a background where women take no interest in finance. She gets an allowance from Joseph and has never set eyes on his bank or credit card statements. So she doesn't see details of meals in London restaurants and small gifts that never find their way to her. She is also unaware of his earnings, believing him when he tells her they have to save money. She doesn't know that they can live well enough on the concerts he does in London and that part of his fees is going towards paying for the trips to Europe.

*

Carla doesn't share many of her thoughts with Joseph. During the daytime he is always preoccupied with his music, playing a passage over and over. He is working on a piece that he says is 'a big technical challenge'. For her it is endless repetition. She wants him to get on to the next part, the Polish dance, but instead he is 'loosening his hands' on trills that he plays a dozen times.

At night she lies awake while he is in a deep sleep. She has a lump on her thumb. It feels hard. She has no idea what it could be, but it doesn't look normal, not the result of a cut or scratch. The nail on her big toe is discoloured; she's read somewhere that this can be a pointer to skin cancer. Then there's the rash under her arm that's only been visible for a week. She once knew someone who had cancer of the armpit; she should make an appointment to see the doctor. She's stopped telling Joseph about her fears. If only she could talk more to her mother, but the cost of calls abroad is too high, and they are trying to save money. So a few days later she is in the surgery, waiting her turn. She shows the doctor the redness under her arm. He agrees that the skin is inflamed, but assures her it's not life threatening.

"Stop using a perfumed deodorant," he says, abruptly.

When Joseph goes abroad to do a concert, he always returns with a small gift. Most men don't know how to buy presents for women, choosing overbright lingerie or ear rings that are too heavy. Joseph seems to have a knack of buying something unusual that looks as if it has come from a designer store, but is probably quite cheap. She wonders when he has time to go shopping as these trips are short. He always leaves London a couple of days before a concert—he wouldn't want to risk any problems with aircraft and bad weather. Then he must find somewhere to practise. After the performance he comes straight home. So Carla is even more appreciative of the effort he has taken to go and buy something just for her.

While he's away she misses him, of course, but it is blissfully quiet in the flat. She puts on some of her old CDs and makes a note that she really will make an effort to go to the Italian church in Clerkenwell. Most nights she goes to sleep early and stretches out over the whole width of the king-size bed.

She sometimes dreams of what it would have been like, if they'd stayed in Italy. She would get on well with her mother-in-law—a sweet woman who believes that gossip is harmful. She often says it's like ripping open a down pillow, and then trying to get the feathers back. Carla imagines them living in the old part of Arezzo, opening the shutters on every sun-filled day, buying vegetables in the market and spending the warm evenings strolling through the streets, stopping to admire her friends' babies, dressed in fine embroidered clothes.

Whenever she mentions such things to Joseph, he gets angry, probably because he knows he would like it too. But he pretends that there's no work for him there and that he is far more successful playing in London halls with his agent finding him occasional engagements abroad.

Carla's English is improving. She can enjoy television and read the headlines in the papers. Some things are more challenging, like the reviews of Joseph's concerts. She can't understand every word, but it's clear that the critics think his performances are first-class. He'll soon be as famous as Alfred Brendel or even the Japanese woman he speaks about: Mitsuko something. She has to concede that he probably wouldn't be doing as well if they'd lived in Italy. Coming to London was a good move—at least for him.

CHAPTER 16

They are on their way to Florence. For once Joseph has agreed to take Carla with him, so she can go on to Arezzo, to see her family. Sophie is installed in the Grand Hotel Cavour with a cool terrace overlooking the rooftops near Dante's house. As usual she is in splendid surroundings and he will be in a cheaper hotel. She has found one called the Cimabue and has promised to wait for him there. He hasn't told her about travelling with Carla—only that he'll arrive in the afternoon so they can have several hours together.

His last text message from Sophie mentioned that she might be able to skip dinner with Tom. There's a cellar at their hotel where residents can turn up later in the evening for tastings of cheese and cold meats.

Joseph and Carla arrive at the airport and he expects to put her on the train to Arezzo. Instead she asks:

"I come to see your hotel first?"

"It's hardly worth it. Your train's in about an hour, isn't it? Anyway, I have to find somewhere to practise. The concert is tomorrow."

"But I could just come and see where you are staying."

The journey to the city centre is only five kilometres and he finds himself agreeing to take Carla to the Cimabue. By the time they arrive he is already wondering what to do. They both know there are several trains a day to Arezzo. As they walk into the lounge he is feeling sick. It begins in his stomach, moving up to his throat. He is swallowing to keep it down, holding his breath to make it go away. He begins to feel unsteady and moves from one foot to another to keep his balance. His hand goes up to wipe away drops of sweat from his forehead. Carla looks at him and must see that he is looking pale. She suggests that they sit down. In front of the sofa is a table with a triangular flower arrangement. Joseph fixes his eyes on it until he feels steady enough to stand again. He moves towards the door where a rush of cold air brings some colour back to his face. After a few minutes he walks over to the reception desk to check in. He hands in his passport slowly, engaging the owner in a conversation about the building, part of a 19th century palazzo. After a few minutes he's handed a key.

"Numero 7, secondo piano".

"I think we should go and have a coffee. It's the heat. I don't feel too good."

"But Joseph, what you mean heat? It's June, what you expect? We're in Italy."

"I've been so long in England I forget what it's like. I can't take it now. I just want to sit down."

"Well, let's go to your room. Maybe I should stay with you a few days before I go to see my parents?"

"No, cara, I'll be working."

"But it would be different here. I promise not to stop you practising. I'm not very nice, sometimes, am I?"

"You're as nice as I deserve."

Before she can comment he begins to walk towards the lift. Carla is following, her high heels clicking on the marble floor.

"Eh, Joseph, you know I don't want to go in the lift."

How could he have forgotten? Of course she would prefer to take the stairs. She is nervous about enclosed spaces and lifts in particular. She begins to climb and he walks behind as she puffs up the steps, her short legs bare in the summer heat. They arrive at the second floor and walk past rooms 4, 5 and 6. As they approach number 7, he takes her arm and turns her round.

"I ... I've forgotten something" he mumbles, ushering her back downstairs.

"What ... where are we going?" she protests, clattering down the stairs again.

He goes to the desk and asks the receptionist if there is anything for him. The man turns his back, runs his hand along the row of small wooden boxes and pulls a package out of the pigeonhole marked with the number 7. He puts it on the desk. Joseph passes it to Carla and breathes out slowly:

"I forgot, cara, I've got something for you. I want to give it to you before you go. I bought it when I was in Bologna last month, and got them to send it here."

Carla opens the box and takes out a necklace with a heart, studded with opals. She throws her arms round his neck and covers him with kisses. She is still thanking him when he extricates his arm to look at his watch.

"We'd better go. You're going to miss your train."

They leave the hotel, walking briskly, with him pulling the suitcase and Carla taking little steps to keep up with him. The walk is longer than he expected. After about ten minutes they arrive at the station. He buys a ticket, finds the right platform and puts her on the train. As it pulls away he raises his arm to wave.

When he gets back to the hotel it's late afternoon. He takes the lift to the second floor and opens the door to his room. It's small, too full of furniture. There's a dark oak chest of drawers and an antique bed with a high bedhead. Sophie is lying naked under the heavy maroon cover. He leans over to kiss her and steadies himself on the bed.

"Joseph, why are you shaking?"

"I'll tell you later."

"What's the matter? You look awful. I know, you forgot my birthday."

"No, I didn't."

"Come on. I don't mind. I didn't really expect you to get me anything."

"Well I did buy you a present, but it's a long story."

Sophie has no idea of how near Carla came to discovering her in Joseph's bed. She misreads his nervousness for concern over his concert arrangements. This leaves her imagination free to explore a quite different scenario: that Tom is about to stumble on her lies and deceptions. Has he ever wondered how she spends her days? Does he not care that in the evenings she prefers to snuggle up with food from Room Service rather than dress up and go out for dinner? Has he noticed the extra kisses she plants on his mouth after a day of 'shopping' or the excuses she makes for sliding away from him in bed? The details are all in place: the museum alibis, the clothes 'purchased' in the city where they are staying, but maybe, just maybe Tom has glimpsed a change in Sophie's behaviour.

For every hour of lovemaking—as sweet as any honeymoon—there are minutes of dark conversations between Sophie and Joseph. Fear and guilt and complaint and annoyance bubble to the surface and boil over in exchanges that leave them both unsettled. They each return to their separate lives in London, but within days they are whispering on the phone and texting sweet loving notes to tide them over till their next meeting. On just one occasion, while Carla is in Arezzo, Sophie comes to the flat in Braganza Street. After she leaves—well before nightfall—Joseph washes the bedsheets and tidies the rooms as if he were a criminal hiding evidence of the tiniest blood stain.

Yet, in spite of the guilt and uncertainty a new confidence emerges. Joseph begins to think they are invincible.

CHAPTER 17

Carla spends two weeks in Arezzo after leaving Joseph in Florence. Her parents live on the second floor of an old building in a cobbled street. She stretches out the days sitting with her mother, shelling the fresh cannellini beans for the ribollita, beating and skinning octopus, and mincing the pork for ragù. Her brother sometimes brings in a rabbit and sits down to eat with them at the wooden table. In the afternoons Carla goes with her father to a bar in the square and if they don't have ice cream, they have a pine nut pastry with their coffee. After ten days of eating leisurely meals twice a day, Carla is putting on weight. Her mother, who is also short and inclined to be shaped like a meatball, a polpetto, reassures her that a rounded bottom and breasts are healthy.

On the third Sunday in June the city will be heaving with tourists who have come to see the Giostra del Saraceno—a jousting competition. Preparations begin weeks before the show. The Piazza Grande is transformed into an arena and the buildings are decked with the flags of the competing teams. The whole town is heaving to the sound and smell of the horses, parading up the side streets past cafe owners who are trying to keep the cobble stones clean. On the day of the dress rehearsal the symbolic Saracen is in place. One by one the riders thunder past on horseback, aiming a pole at metal head, trying to avoid being hit by the swinging ball and chain attached to the Saracen's arm. But this year the police are expecting trouble. There are enough Muslims in the town to object to the whole idea of the Giostra. Cafes off the square have been told to remove the cutlery from the tables and the restaurants in the Colonnade will hide the china and bring out plastic plates. In case of a riot, it's wise to limit the available ammunition.

Carla leaves her home town before the tourists arrive. She has had a dozen conversations with Joseph about the return flight and has finally agreed that she'll do it alone. On June 17th her father takes her to the airport and holds her hand till he has to wave her through the departure gate. She clutches her passport dreading the moment when she will walk up the steps to the plane. Once her seatbelt is fastened she is trying to concentrate, telling herself that she's doing this for Joseph. In truth, she knows it's for herself, to prove that she is capable of conquering her nerves. The belt feels too tight, pressing on her stomach. Carla grips the seat handles, squeezing so tight that the call button begins to flash. When the steward appears, she is confused and apologetic:

"No, va bene. I'm sorry. Is OK."

He brings her a glass of water, concerned that she is far from OK. She takes a few sips and then pulls out a magazine. She must know that there is little to see from the window, but just in case, she keeps her eyes straight ahead, fearful of looking down and realising how far an aeroplane has to fall out of the sky before it comes crashing to the ground. The tension in her neck turns to a pain. She searches in her bag for the panino with prosciutto that her mother has packed for her. She is just finishing the sandwich when the plane begins its descent. At Gatwick Carla makes her way through customs and says she has four bottles of olive oil to declare. By the time she reaches the baggage area her old leather suitcase is already trundling round the carousel. Joseph is there to meet her and together they begin the long journey to Kennington.

"So, how is your father? Did he talk about me?"

"You've never forgiven him, have you?"

"Well, I can hardly forget what he called me. Did he ask about the monster?"

"No, I think he was just pleased to see me. You know he didn't mean it. He didn't want you to take me away."

"Sure. But now he could be pleased. He could be happy that I've got bookings, that we have a good life in London."

"He would have been happier if you'd worked in a butcher's shop in Arezzo."

"Or if you'd married that one-eyed postino who kept stuffing the letters in his pockets. He really was a monster."

They are both tired as they drag the case along Braganza Street, past all the identical terraced houses and into their flat. The rooms look strangely tidy and Joseph's clothes are folded in piles, instead of being strewn across chairs and stools.

"It looks like you've had a cleaner here." says Carla.

"No, no. I just thought I'd clear up for you. I missed you."

Joseph puts his arms round her, feeling the heat of her body through the thin cotton top. He lifts it over her head and she wriggles out of the skirt. He moves her towards the bed and begins to run his hands over her body. He doesn't take the time to take off his own clothes and struggles with the zip of his trousers. He enters her with a rush of passion and guilt. Pulling the covers over her, he slides off the bed, fastens his button and belt and turns to kiss the top of her head.

"I have to go, I'm meeting Richard."

*

Carla is unpacking when the phone rings.

"Eh, Richard, he's not here. He's gone to meet you."

"When? We don't have an appointment."

"But he said ..."

"I haven't talked to him for a while. You know he's bad at answering the phone."

"Well, he wasn't here. He was playing in the concert in Florence, but then he was home. It was just me who stayed on."

"Wait a minute. What do you mean, a concert in Florence? He never told me about it."

"He must have done. Didn't you arrange it for him?"

The line goes quiet.

"Richard, are you still there?"

"I don't know about a booking in Florence. He hasn't done any work abroad for months."

"What are you telling me? what about Antwerp and Bologna?"

"I don't know about anything in Europe. He must have arranged them himself."

Carla puts down the phone. The first thought in her mind is that Joseph has probably found a new agent. She can imagine Richard looking tense, pulling out his shirt cuffs, adjusting his bow tie. But Joseph has never discussed his work arrangements with her. Why should it concern her now if he's found someone else to represent him? Reason is telling her one thing, but her fingers are already flicking through the address book to find Richard's number. She immediately calls him back.

"Richard, we need to talk. Can you meet me for a coffee?"

"When, now? Carla, I'm really busy."

"No, Richard, I need talk with you. I see you in that place on the corner, by the newsagent. I'll be there in ten minutes."

She puts the phone down before he can respond. Carla is already sitting at a plastic-topped table when he arrives. She looks up and glances round at the other customers. For some reason she feels awkward, thinking that a man in such tailored clothes is out of place in the sandwich bar.

"What's this all about, Carla?"

Richard has already discovered that Joseph had no booking in Florence. He has checked the concert halls on the internet and found only orchestral music and solo violin and oboe. He asks her about the dates of the other two venues.

"Look, here are the reviews." Carla pulls out some press releases from her handbag.

"How you explain? Look at these. They're all about his performances. Are you telling me he wasn't there? I know he went."

She is too diplomatic to say what is in her mind, that Joseph has found another agent. Richard's silence is beginning to unsettle her.

"Isn't it possible he fixed the concerts himself?" she asks.

Richard doesn't tell her that there were no concerts. He fiddles with his cufflink:

"It's possible. Perhaps he was invited to play and thought he could do without his agent."

He looks at Carla's face and realises she has already come to her own conclusion. She is dabbing at her eyes with a tissue. She hasn't touched the sandwich he's ordered for her. He's embarrassed that people are looking and suggests that they leave and go back to his flat for a drink. He hails a taxi which weaves its way towards Pimlico. It stops outside a newly painted stucco house. He leads her down the steps to the basement.

Richard opens the door and asks her to come in. At one end of the room is a small chest piled with books and a large bed with dark covers. He seems to have no television but an array of hi-fi equipment and CDs stacked to the ceiling. There are no chairs, only a bar stool next to a peninsula in a small area that's been fitted out as a kitchen. Carla is surprised that the bedsit is so small. She'd imagined him living in a spacious flat. But the fashionable postcodes of London mean nothing to her. For Richard it is more important to live in a single room in desirable SW1 than to operate from a large space with an E1 address. Carla is still standing when he pours her a glass of whisky.

"Sit down," he says, straightening out the bed cover.

"What's he doing, Richard? Do you think he's been with someone?"

"Why should you think that? Just because he's fixed up a few concerts doesn't mean he's having an affair. Tell you what, let's look on the internet together and see what they have to say about his concert in Bologna."

One whisky turns into two, then they open a bottle of wine. Richard's attempt to cheer her up has made Carla even more miserable. They find no reference to any piano concerts in Bologna in the past few months. Carla drains her glass and says:

"There you are. It's obvious. If he's not playing in a concert, what is he doing?"

She begins to cling to Richard, sobbing:

"Ma no. How could he do this? What have I done to him? I don't deserve this."

He detaches her arms and goes to fetch a tissue to wipe her tears. He doesn't say anything but puts his hand on the wet patches on her face. Carla's misery and anger turn into a longing for affection and with the effects of the wine, an urge for oblivion.

Richard is sober enough to judge that it would be churlish of him to push her away. He doesn't want to add to her suffering by making her feel doubly rejected. Neither of them has any intention of making love. It just happens.

CHAPTER 18

Carla is overcome with guilt. How can she confront Joseph and accuse him of having a lover when she has done the very same thing? Except that Richard is no lover. He is a huge, ugly, smartly dressed, grinning mistake. Since the afternoon in his flat she is filled with confusion and bitterness. She is furious with Richard for taking advantage of her when she was miserable, and angry with her husband, for whatever it is he has been doing. Every time Joseph picks up the phone she hovers nearby, listening to the conversation. She sneaks a look at his diary. When the post arrives she watches him open each letter and stands there while he takes out music scores and bills. The weeks pass and Carla retreats into a dark silence, imagining a host of illnesses that might be attacking her body.

A heavy, listless tiredness hangs over every day. Even after ten hours sleep she is hardly able to drag herself out of bed in the mornings. While she was never tidy or bustling, a simple task like clearing the table is now postponed and dreaded as if it were a major activity. Any noise triggers a headache and Joseph's repetitive chord-playing makes her agitated to the point when she closes her eyes and wants to scream. But few words come out of her mouth; it's as if the effort is too much. Lethargy turns into depression. Misery settles in her brain, only relieved by daytime naps where she lies in bed with the covers pulled over her head.

She wakes to the sound of Joseph practising a repetitive five notes over and over again. She waits for ten minutes, nervous that any complaint will make him slam down the piano lid and send him rushing out of the room. She holds her breath, walks slowly into the kitchen and makes him a cup of coffee.

For the month of July Joseph is concentrating on his repertoire. He is working at home every day, building up speed and stamina. A technique he'd forgotten from his days as a student in Perugia comes back to him: playing 'horizontally' not 'vertically'. A teacher had shown him how to hold the piano lid a few inches above the keyboard with his left hand, forcing the fingers on the right hand to stay close to the keys. The notes can then be played faster, with less wasted effort lifting the fingers high. He's aiming at a swift, fleeting sound. After he's played the piece twice over, he clicks the playback button to hear the recording, then begins again with the same notes reverberating through the flat, drumming into Carla's ears.

One evening he suggests a walk to get out of the intense heat in the flat. He tells her he's planning a trip in August. They walk past the red brick mansion blocks in De Laune Street and cross the road into Kennington Park. They pass the hairdresser, grandly named Park View. Carla isn't speaking. She's beginning to feel breathless. She says nothing about his time in Florence and lets him chatter on:

"This concert in Lisbon, it's at a place called the Gulbenkian Foundation. I won't get paid because the tickets are free."

She catches the word 'free' and responds crossly:

"And you're going all that way for no money?"

"I have to look ahead. I'm not known in Portugal, so if I want to make a name there, I have to do it."

"So what's so special about Portugal, why you need to go there?"

"Carla, stop it, please. If this concert goes well, they might invite me back for a serious one next year. Have you forgotten? This is how I earn the money to keep us."

She stops to take a stone out of her sandal. He waits. They walk on. They are both looking ahead. Carla is wondering whether to tell him that she knows about his so-called concerts in Europe. She decides to say it was Richard who raised the subject. His response is defensive:

"Since when do you discuss my arrangements with Richard?"

"Since he told me ... he knew nothing. That you went to Belgium or Italy."

Joseph turns to her and the expression on his face is a mixture of exasperation and sorrow:

"Amore. I was going to tell you. I've been planning my own bookings abroad. I've been doing it many times, many months. It's saving us money."

"What do you mean?"

"Well, if I make the arrangements I get the whole fee. If Richard does it, I only get 75%."

Carla wants to believe him. His explanation for the bookings seems plausible. Richard must have been wrong about the concerts in Italy. Only yesterday Joseph pulled out a review, translated into English from Corriere della Sera. She has re-read it several times, delighted that the arts critic thinks so highly of her husband.

When Joseph is with her, smiling and assuring her that he's doing his best for both of them, she believes him. But when she's alone, the depression returns and she is preoccupied with aches in her limbs. Her left arm, particularly, has a nagging pain all along the inside. Doesn't heart trouble begin with a pain in this arm? Carla begins each day with a minute examination of her skin. She usually finds a couple of unexplained blotches or spots. But under the skin there are the minute lumps—little clumps that weren't there yesterday. She checks to see if there is a matching one on the other side of her body. There usually is, so the fears of a possible cancer make way for thoughts of Joseph's infidelity—and her own afternoon of weakness. Five weeks have passed since the humiliation with

Richard. Carla lets the answering machine pick up messages—dreading a conversation with him. Each morning she wakes up and remembers what she's done, but now the shame is mixed with other concerns. She feels heavy and bloated—probably the result of the generous Tuscan diet.

CHAPTER 19

Carla has a small diary bound in Florentine leather. In it she marks her parents' birthdays, her wedding anniversary and the dates of Joseph's concerts. There is also a series of stars and squiggles to remind her of various points in the month. In July there were two squiggles instead of the usual five; now in August she realises there are none at all. She flicks the pages over again and confirms that her period is two days late. The blank dates stare back at her. What seems to be a weight gain brought on by eating may be something quite different. She knows from advertisements on the underground that you can take a home pregnancy test. That must be better than having a doctor putting his fingers in embarrassing places. It's easy to go into a chemist and buy a kit.

She walks to the corner of the street and goes into the shop. The girl behind the counter smiles at her. Carla picks up a bottle of shampoo and takes it to the till, leaving without buying the one thing she needs. The next day she takes the train to Oxford Street and goes into a large chain store, buzzing with office workers buying lunchtime sandwiches. At the checkout Carla hides the kit under a pack of cotton wool balls. You never know who might be looking.

For a week the test kit stays under the purse in the handbag. Finally Carla returns from a shopping trip, lifts it out and throws the bag on to a chair. In the bathroom her hands are shaking as she reads the instructions. No-one is in the flat to hear the faint trickle or to see the expression on her face when a blue line appears in the test window: the result is positive. There are no friends to confide in. It's too early to tell Joseph or to speak to her mother, as she needs confirmation from a doctor. Maybe the kit is unreliable and there's been a mistake?

In the doctor's surgery the conversation quickly moves to a calculation of dates. It seems that Carla has conceived around the 18th June, just after her return from Arezzo. The baby is due on 10th March.

Carla stares at the telephone and dials the code for Italy. She imagines her mother at the other end, in the kitchen, wiping the flour off her arms, putting down the long rolling pin she uses to make the pasta. She'll run to tell the neighbours and within days she'll start knitting—a white shawl in finest wool. Her father will be happy. He's often dropped hints about a grandchild; how he hopes she won't leave it till he's too old. Carla has almost forgiven him for the way he behaved to Joseph. His comment that she was 'on loan' was a sign of his affection for her, nothing else. There have been times when she's considered—just for a moment—going back to Arezzo for a while, leaving the grey skies in England. But she can't imagine being without Joseph. It is unthinkable.

Her parents are overjoyed. Her mother asks if she's eating properly and whether she has a good doctor. Her father can't resist a dig at her husband:

"He'd better not play the piano in the evenings. It'll keep the baby awake."

Carla is relieved to have told them the news. There's another person who might want to know, but after so many years of marriage, it's hardly a thing to blurt out, without careful thought. That's why she doesn't tell Joseph immediately. It will come as a shock; he's always assumed she was on the pill. How is she going to tell him that for a few days around her return from Italy, the fear of the flight put all thoughts of taking the pills out of her mind? And how is he going to take it? Will he be pleased? After their wedding they talked about having babies and Joseph said he wanted six. Carla thought she was too young and made him agree to put it off till they were more settled. Settled? How can she feel stable when depression is floating like a black cloud over everything? How can she think of having a baby when she can hardly take care of herself?

Carla wakes up each day, feeling her spreading waistline and wishing that instead of a baby inside, it was the result of too much pasta and pastries. But at least the pregnancy takes her mind off her other fears about her health.

In the past year there have been at least two concerns that prompted a visit to the doctor: the 'cancer of the armpit' scare, and an itching eyelid, surely an indication of an imminent loss of eyesight. But now, the only real symptom she has is nausea, not just in the mornings when it might be expected, but every time she pictures Richard's grinning face.

There's something distasteful about him; his hairless body and the perfectly smooth skin. Not a word has passed between them since that dreadful afternoon. It was all because of the chairs—or lack of them. How can a man live in a flat without an armchair? If she'd been able to sit down she would never have ended up on the bed. Carla decides she is going to block it out of her mind. She won't let her thoughts dwell on the embarrassment of finding herself in his bed, putting on her pants and shoes, rushing up the steps and out into the street. As for the possibility of Richard being the father of her baby, it is too horrific to contemplate. There's certainly no need to discuss it with him; it won't have entered his mind. Of course they didn't use a condom as he would have assumed she was taking precautions. By the time her pregnancy is obvious he will be out of their lives. If Joseph has been planning his own concerts, he must either have another agent already, or he'll be doing it himself. Either way he won't need Richard any more.

At times Carla is thinking clearly, but she has managed to ignore the most obvious truth: if Joseph wasn't playing in concerts abroad, he must have been doing something. Carla has brought on a self-inflicted blindness, blocking out the mystery of Joseph's trips.

In the case of true blindness, the solution is to adapt. Carla has a friend who lost her sight and has learned how to do this. She fixes textured tape on to navy trousers to distinguish them from the black pair; she's learned to make tea in a mug, using a battery-operated liquid level indicator, which sits on top of the cup and beeps when the hot liquid touches the prongs. Neighbours help her read the post that comes thudding on to the doormat every morning. For the rest of the day she learns to forget that she can't see. In the same way Carla simply closes her eyes to the possibility of Joseph's infidelity and channels her thoughts in another direction: that he is doing his best for them. She tells herself that she is having his baby and they're going to be happy.

Before breaking the news Carla waits until Joseph is in a good mood. Apparently he's anxious about a package that hasn't come.

"Carla, have you seen a parcel with some sheet music? I'm expecting a Mozart Fantasia from a new supplier."

"No, but I opened something for you the other day. It was a big package, but it wasn't music."

"What was it?"

"I don't know. It was some catalogue from a museo. They must have sent it to the wrong person. I think I threw it away."

He looks worried. He obviously can't get on with the piece until the music arrives. When he's got started on the Fantasia she'll tell him about the baby. Even though it's not what they planned, he's sure to be pleased.

*

Chapter 20

The flat is back to the usual chaos. In those brief days after Sophie came to his bed, Joseph had wiped away any sign or clue that he might not have been alone. Now he is wondering, yet again, how he ever got himself into this situation.

It's not a fling, not a passing affair. Sophie is always in his thoughts. It started from the first moment he saw her. It's not just the beautiful calm face or the voice. She uses fewer words than Carla, doesn't chatter or criticize, but talks about his work and seems endlessly interested in learning more about music and the techniques of playing it. Carla has never shown the slightest wish to hear him play in public, but Sophie is always there, sitting at the side, out of his line of vision, waiting to discuss every missed note. She also watches the audience, telling him later how they reacted to different parts of the programme and which encore was most popular.

When they are alone together—for an hour in a cafe or an afternoon in a darkened hotel room—it's as if the stress in his life has been filtered out with the world beyond the shutters. The love he feels for Sophie obliterates the concert nerves and the irritations of living with a wife who doesn't understand him.

Carla is talking about the weather. They could be two strangers on a train except that her remarks are barbed. Her complaints begin about the grey skies but quickly turn to an attack on him, for bringing her to this infernal climate.

"Joseph, I hate England."

"What you mean? Why are you starting this now?"

"You know what I mean. Half the year everything is dull. I feel like I need to turn a switch to make the colour come on. It's not like this in Arezzo."

"Of course it's not. And there's no work in Arezzo."

"That's not what I say."

"You do. You're depressed because of the weather. But what you're really saying is that I leave you alone too much."

"It's you.You say it. Not me."

"Let's leave it, Carla. I have to practise."

Joseph needs to perfect his fingering of the Mozart but instead his hands roll into the theme from the film Cinema Paradiso. He lets his mind wander and dreams about being on stage with a full orchestra behind him. He is so carried away he can almost imagine having composed the piece himself. Carla comes into the room carrying a glass and she sits down to sip the clear liquid. When the last note fades away he turns to ask what she's drinking. It's some kind of infusion.

Joseph is not totally hard-hearted. He realises how annoying it is when he locks himself into a world that excludes Carla. He strokes her face and asks:

"Why didn't you wait? I'd have made you some coffee."

"I don't want any. The smell makes me feel bad."

"What do you mean? You've always loved coffee."

"But now it makes me feel sick—even thinking about it."

"Carla, you're getting a bit fussy. First it was parmesan, now it's coffee. What's wrong with you? "

"Joseph, I have something to tell you."

"Can't it wait? I have to get back to the Mozart."

"What would you say if ... if I forgot to take the pill for one or two days?"

"I don't know. Well, you wouldn't forget. You have the pack by the bed. You take one every day."

"But what if I didn't and missed a day or two?"

"Well, then I suppose you might get pregnant."

He stops and looks at her. She is twisting the curl behind her ear.

"Ehi. Un attimo. Che cosa? What are you telling me?"

He starts coughing, spitting out drops of black coffee on to the kitchen table. His eyes are watering too. By the time Carla has patted his back and waited for his voice to come out without a squeak, Joseph has recovered.

"Are you OK?"

"Me? I'm fine."

"Say you're pleased, Joseph. Say something."

"Look, I've got coffee all over the table."

"Joseph. What do you think? I know we didn't expect it."

"Well, I don't know what to say. It's a surprise."

"Yes, but now it's happened, say you're happy."

"Carla, I don't have to say it. You know I love babies."

"But you look so shocked."

"No, it's just the timing. I've got this concert planned. It's not just the Mozart. I have to put together a programme."

Carla is wiping the table. She's unusually quiet. He goes back to the piano and for the twentieth time begins the Mozart Fantasia. It opens with a minor key flourish and has a dark, dramatic mood. Carla is mumbling in the background as he goes over and over the seemingly impossible fingering. Mozart wants the player's right hand to strike the keys forty-nine separate times in bar 84. Joseph goes back again and again, turning the pages and repeating the demisemiquavers.

He is trying to use the music to calm his mind and blot out the images of Sophie laughing as she invents his reviews and Carla worrying about the minutest details of her life. Strangest of all is the thought that he is going to be a father; that in some months (he'd forgotten to ask how many) Carla would be lying on a hospital bed, pushing a bambino out into this world of confusion.

He still can't get out of his mind the fiasco in Florence when Carla was within a whisper of discovering Sophie in his hotel room. On that day he felt he was having a heart attack, with all the classic symptoms—shortness of breath, feeling sick, shooting pains. Looking back this was an attack of a different kind—panic at the thought of what was about to happen.

So now Joseph is careful. He is surprised that Carla never pressed him about the concerts abroad, believing his explanation that he no longer needs an agent. He deletes messages from his phone, throws away credit card bills and only meets Sophie for brief moments before or after a concert in London. Leisurely meals in a restaurant might need an explanation so he spends more time at home, practising. Since Carla has added cigarettes to the list of things that make her feel sick, he has to go outside for a smoke and it's in those moments that he whispers messages to Sophie while they plan their next encounter.

As he prepares for his trip to Lisbon Joseph has more than the music to worry about. Sophie has been texting him with details of his accommodation. Any hotel with a name like 'The Comfort' has to be small and run-down and Joseph is beginning to feel disgruntled at the prospect. While he's trying to master the dramatic shifts in the Fantasia he is constantly wondering how to tell Sophie about the baby. How will she react? This has to be the last time they are away together. Perhaps they can carry on meeting in London? They once discussed the idea of him coming to her flat in Maida Vale. The suggestion came from him:

"I could just stay for an hour or so."

"But I'd be on edge all the time."

"Why? Because of Tom? He's always out in the day."

"Yes, but just think about it. Say he forgot something and came back to get it."

Joseph is imagining the sound of Tom's key turning in the lock while he hides under the bedclothes. It's a farce he can't begin to contemplate. He has to work out a more sensible course. Perhaps he'll be able to find a practice studio where he can take Sophie for the afternoon. One part of his brain is telling him he can continue leading a double life; the other says he has no choice—he has to end it.

CHAPTER 21

Joseph arrives at the Comfort Hotel Embaixador—a ten storey building on a corner. Far from the small place he imagined, it looks like a faded ocean liner. His single room has sound-proofed windows and has been recently redecorated. The contract must have gone to the lowest bidder; within a year the paint on the walls will be peeling again. He takes the lift down to the ground floor and walks out into a wide avenue. Sophie would have noted the name—Avenida Duque de Loule—and known that the park he is passing through is named after Edward VII. He walks north past a statue and makes his way to the concert hall in the Gulbenkian complex. He's keen to make the final arrangements for his concert on Sunday. At the office a secretary smiles at him:

"You must have an admirer. Someone telephoned to ask when you are performing."

"Someone phoned? For me? From where?"

"I don't know. London, I think. She was speaking English but sounded foreign. Maybe she's one of your fans."

"And what did you say to her?"

"I told her about our free concerts and that you're on the list."

*

This time it's not Joseph who is kept waiting. Sophie is sitting in the lobby of the Comfort Hotel, with a map of Lisbon in her hand. She looks up every time a guest walks through the doors. She runs her fingers through her hair, shakes it loose and twists it into a coil, letting it fall again as she keeps her eye on the entrance. Finally he arrives and they go up to his room. He slots in the card but the door won't open. They wait in silence as he turns it over and tries the other way. The green light flashes and they go in.

"Where were you? I've been waiting for two hours."

"I had to find somewhere to practise. Sophie, you don't realise. This is the first time I've had the distraction of a real concert. I can't think about us till I've got the Fantasia right."

"It's funny how it worked out. I did try to invent a booking for you. I found out about two venues: the Teatro Camões and the Teatro Nacional."

Joseph seems preoccupied but she continues:

"But because it's August there's not much going on. It was lucky you heard about the free concerts."

Sophie is tugging at the zip of her silk dress. She slides it off her shoulders and stands there, waiting for him to unfasten the clip on her bra. He's fiddling with a handkerchief as he doesn't want to touch her with his cold, clammy hands. She starts to pull her dress up again and only then does he move towards her, wrapping his arms around her, stroking the long strands of hair. She can't see his face.

"Sophie ... I ... amore, I'm sorry I was late."

"Don't worry, it doesn't matter. I understand."

He steps back and pushes the handkerchief in his pocket.

"You've no idea how hard this programme is. And I have to make an impression. I feel like my fingers are stuck together."

"I think I liked it better when I arranged the concerts."

Joseph tries to smile.

"Tom is going to Venice at the end of October. I've never been in a gondola. I can't wait."

"It isn't the weather for Venice. It's cold in the autumn."

"But it's a good time to go. There won't be any crowds."

"The canals ... it's so damp at that time of year."

"Joseph, don't you want to come?"

"I do, but I'm not sure if I can."

"What do you mean? It's two months away. You haven't got a booking in London have you?"

"No, not exactly, but there's something."

"What is it? what are you trying to say?"

"Nothing. Sophie, come here. We haven't got that long today because I have to be at the concert hall early."

"No. Tell me. You were about to say something."

Joseph takes a deep breath, practising the relaxation technique he uses before a performance.

"Maybe ..." He closes his eyes and lets the words rush out:

"Perhaps it would be better if ... if we don't see each other quite so much."

"But why?"

"I don't know. I ..."

She doesn't let him finish.

"Well, if that's how you feel."

She is fingering her hair and her eyes are blinking. She straightens her dress and pushes him away from her, mumbling:

"I'll see you tomorrow. I'll leave you to practise."

"Sophie, listen. We've got to talk."

He's planned to tell her about Carla but his thoughts are racing like a speeding car on a motorway suddenly faced with a hold-up. He watches as she slips into the high heeled sandals, feels the brush of her lips against his face and stands, rooted, as she walks to the door. He doesn't see her disappearing into a bathroom, emerging ten minutes later, dabbing her face with a tissue.

CHAPTER 22

Tom is working with the owner of a small hotel in Lisbon called the Metropole. It's a turn of the century building that looks like a private house from the 1920s. It has antique furniture and spectacular views of the castle. He's managed to persuade the owner to include some modern works of art and has commissioned a photographer to produce black and white pictures of single fruits. When the framed photos arrive Tom is shocked to see that they are not of the pears he'd ordered, but are slices of watermelon. The lack of colour makes the sections look like half moons, with none of the juiciness associated with the red flesh of the fruit.

They are staying at the Ritz. Sophie is excited about the down pillows, the enormous bath and the view over the Eduardo VII park. On the first day she's happy and excited at the prospect of shopping in the boutiques in Bairro Alto. They've brought with them a tourist guide describing the 17th century houses with wrought iron balconies and walls painted in yellow and pink. Sophie is only interested in the clothes.

"You know there's this designer called Nuno Gama and I've found out about the places to go. Here it is, on this bit of paper: there's a shop called Gardenia in Rua Nova do Almado Chiado."

"Sorry, what did you say, Sophie?"

"Nothing, I was just telling you where I'm going shopping."

He's not listening to her attempts at pronouncing Portuguese street names. All he can think about is what to say to the photographer. He wonders if he can get copies of the pear photograph that he'd originally wanted, or whether he'll be stuck with the watermelon slices. For once he envies Sophie the carefree day ahead of her, with nothing to contend with, apart from paying for a new outfit in euros.

*

In the evening Tom comes back to the Ritz to find Sophie curled up on the bed watching the shopping channel on television. He starts to tell her about his meeting with the photographer and goes on about pears or watermelons and numbers of pictures.

"It sounds like you didn't have a good day." she says, hardly taking her eyes off the screen.

"I didn't. How about you?"

"It was OK."

"Where do you want to go for dinner?"

"I don't want to go out. Let's just order something in."

A waiter brings a tray with a bottle of wine and a chef's salad. Sophie picks at the slices of meat and then pushes her plate away. She walks to the window and looks out across the park. Tom is behind her, with his hand on her shoulder.

"... and I suppose you've bought something cutting edge. What's the trend at the moment? Silk and chiffon or strongly defined shapes?"

"Tom, you're being sarcastic again. I'm going to get ready for bed."

*

The next day Sophie is still in a strange mood. Tom suggests they have lunch together as his meeting might be over by mid-day.

"It's too hot."

"But we have to eat. I've heard there's a place that does wonderful bacalhau. Why don't we go there?"

Sophie is pulling a thin blouse over her head.

"I couldn't. I really couldn't face it. I'm not sure I like salted dried cod at the best of times, but in this temperature?"

"Well, we don't have to eat that. We could have roasted shrimp with garlic."

"Tom, I can't think about food at this time in the morning. Why don't we just have dinner in the hotel restaurant this evening?"

She goes out leaving Tom to pick up his papers. His meeting does finish early and when he gets back at midday he finds a brown bag on the bed. This isn't any ordinary paper bag. It has the words Emporio Armani in black and has handles made from twisted cord. He never usually notices, but he's surprised that she hasn't bought something from the Portuguese designer, the one she's been talking about. He looks inside and finds a soft tailored charcoal jacket. The bill is from Bond Street, London. Why would Sophie have bought a bag from a London store to Lisbon? Underneath the bill are two more snippets of paper. One has a phone number: The Comfort Hotel Embaixador, Lisbon, with a note 'close to Marques de Pombal and Ed VII park'. The other sheet also has Sophie's handwriting: 'Orquestra Sinfonica Portuguesa—Teatro Camões, Parque das Nacaos. Classical—Teatro Nacional de Sao Carlos'. What does it mean? They're not planning to go to any concerts—they just have dinner together in the evenings.

CHAPTER 23

Sophie has left the Ritz in a hurry. She's taken more than the usual trouble with lip-liner and mascara and chosen a pair of flowing trousers with a chiffon top in a toning green print. Not knowing what time she'll be back, she's already thought of leaving her 'shopping' in the room. Of course, she's brought it with her, so all that's needed is for her to lift the Armani bag out of the suitcase and leave it on the bed. In her haste and concern about Joseph's nervous mood, she doesn't remember to take out the bill and the notes she's written.

At the Comfort Hotel Sophie walks slowly to Joseph's room. She hesitates before knocking on the door. She's hardly had any sleep; going over and over the words he said. He has also had a sleepless night, dreading the imminent confrontation. He opens the door, takes her hand and begins to talk rapidly. His face is contorted and in spite of the August heat his fingers feel like ice.

"What is it, darling? Tell me."

"I don't know where to begin."

"Has something happened? Has Carla found out?"

"No, it's worse than that."

"What could be worse?"

"She's pregnant."

Sophie is staring at him. Her mouth won't open. Words are forming in the back of her throat but they won't come out. After a moment she mumbles:

"She can't be."

"I tell you, she is."

"She's probably imagining it. You told me she's a bit of a hypochondriac. It'll turn out to be nothing."

"Amore, I tell you, it's true."

The room is swimming. Joseph is kissing her and stroking her hair.

"How could you?"

She punches his chest, poking him with her fingers, pushing him back so that he falls on to the bed.

"You promised. You said she didn't mean anything to you."

Joseph gets up and walks to the window. He turns to face her.

"But Sophie, you knew. We both knew. You were making love with Tom. I didn't want Carla to suspect anything."

"But we agreed. We stopped. I haven't slept with Tom for months."

"It wasn't a regular thing. Carla was depressed. If we hadn't ... you know ... she would have suspected something."

Sophie takes off her shoe and hurls it at him. It catches the side of his face.

"You ... you beast. How could you? I loved you. You promised."

"Sophie, stop it, please."

He comes towards her, holding out his arms. There are drops of blood falling from the broken skin on his cheek. He tries to pull her towards him and lowers his head to kiss her throat. She pushes him away, shouting:

"I expect you're chuffed about it. A little bambino for Carla and Joseph."

The reference to an Italian baby makes him defensive. He delivers a barb that's aimed to hurt Sophie as much as the wound she's opened on his face.

"But you never wanted a child."

"No, I didn't."

Joseph is straightening his hair. How can he have been so cruel? The look on her face is deflated and infinitely sad. She looks straight at him and whispers:

"... and I particularly don't want Carla to have your child."

For a moment neither of them speaks. The blood from Joseph's face has made blotches on Sophie's chiffon blouse. She turns to him with a look of bewilderment:

"We had something special. Don't say we didn't. It had nothing to do with children. It was how we felt about each other."

"And that hasn't changed. Amore, I promise."

"There you go again, with your promises."

"Look at it from my point of view for a minute. I need time to think."

Sophie is silent. She puts on one shoe and starts to look around for the other one. Joseph seems to be floundering, holding up his hands:

"Listen, I won't be able to disappear every month to come and meet you, but we can work something out. Perhaps it's all for the best."

The trite sentences he's delivered are his attempt to extricate himself. What does he mean 'it's for the best'? The thought of losing her brings a stab of pain to his chest. He is willing her to read his thoughts, but with no word from him, no gesture, it's as if he is twisting a knife in her heart.

They look at each other in silence. She takes care to conceal the true extent of her misery, having released the anger but none of the devastation.

"Yes, of course. It's certainly best for you. And me? It would be a bit dramatic if I said it was the end."

Sophie seems confused and withdrawn when she comes back to the hotel. Tom has already changed into comfortable clothes.

"Come on Sophie baby. Let's go out."

"I don't feel like it."

She is slipping off her blouse and goes straight to the bathroom.

"Well, if we're not going out you don't need to change."

"I'm not. I've got something on it. I just need to wash it off."

Tom follows her into the bathroom where she is dabbing at some spots on the shoulder.

"I'm not sure if this chiffon is washable".

The water in the basin has turned a dull red. She leaves the blouse soaking in the basin. A few minutes later she goes back and the green from the print has run into the murky water.

"Oh God, now look what I've done. I'm so stupid. What did I do that for? I can't do anything right."

"What are you talking about?

Her face is taut and she turns away from him.

"What is it?"

"It's nothing. I'm OK."

Tom goes to put his arm round her.

"It's just a blouse. I expect you've got plenty more."

She pushes him away and yells:

"Don't start that again."

"Whoa, whoa, Sophie, what's up? I'm just trying to understand why you're so upset."

She is looking through the drawers for something else to wear. She doesn't go through the pile but picks out the one that's on top. Even he can see that it doesn't go with her trousers. He tries again, speaking quietly:

"Anyway, do you want to show me what you got?"

Tom nods towards the bag on the bed.

"Oh, that. Not really."

"Sophie, what's up? You don't even want to show me what you've bought. That's not like you. You're always so happy when we're away together. I thought you enjoyed coming with me?"

"I ... I just don't feel very well. I'm probably getting a cold."

She disappears into the bathroom. When she comes out she's wiping her eyes and the towel is wet. She may have been washing but she never uses water on her face; she uses some sort of cream and cotton wool. It looks as if she's been crying.

CHAPTER 24

After the concert in Lisbon Joseph goes home on the next flight. He can't stop thinking of the triangle in his life: how he has succeeded in hurting both the wife he is committed to and the woman he loves. To take his mind off the thought of the tears and anger, he convinces himself that his trips abroad weren't always filled with guilt and introspection. Sophie has changed his whole perspective, lifting him out of a dull routine, reminding him how to laugh. Even in a seedy hotel, with a small bed and a shower that drizzled cold, then boiling water, they could make each other happy.

Every time she phones it's like a spark that brings him to life again, but after that day in Lisbon and the shock of their first and only row, they don't see each other for a few weeks. They've agreed to speak again when they've both calmed down. He only waits a couple of days before he sends her a text. She replies with a sentence that makes him call back immediately. Before long they are in daily contact again. They find somewhere to meet—a bar near the National Gallery, in a hotel called The Trafalgar, convenient as an alibi for her looking at paintings or for him playing at St. Martin in the Fields. But there's no one to see them. They've found a table in a dark corner away from the bustle around the bar.

There's no question of taking a room at the hotel—it's far too expensive. And both of them seem to have come to their senses, realising that they have no future together, yet they are unable to break it off completely. Throughout September and October they meet twice a week, saying little, touching each other's hands as they reach for a drink. They have a tacit agreement to keep the conversation light, with no mention of Carla or Tom, but with each passing week, the date of the birth comes closer, like a train hurtling towards a closed level crossing.

The streets of London are adorned with glitter and crowds jostle in and out of the stores, looking for Christmas presents. As the holiday draws nearer the search for the perfect gift becomes more frantic. The Trafalgar is filled with men and women in their twenties, happy that they've finally made a choice. As he waits for Sophie to arrive Joseph listens to the conversation around him. A woman holding up a pink tie asks her friend:

"Do you think he'll like it?"

"It's awesome."

Joseph looks at the hideous tie and can imagine the 'oohs' and 'aahs' when the paper is unwrapped. Will it ever be worn or will it be stuffed in the back of a drawer, one of the millions of unwanted gifts bought in December and forgotten in January?

Sophie comes in and walks past the couples standing near the bar. The music is louder than usual but changes suddenly to an emotional ballad. A guitar is playing the instrumental melody.

She puts both arms round him and holds him close:

"Know what it is? Very apt. It's Sonata Arctica. It's called The Misery."

He can hear snatches of the words:

"Can't we be together, without them forever ... if you fall, I'll catch."

After a few minutes of trying to talk over the music, she slides something across the table towards him and whispers in his ear:

"You always told me I'd like him."

"Who?"

"Mitsuko, remember?"

Joseph laughs and pulls off the wrapping. Inside is a box of Mitsuko Uchida CDs. He turns it over then leans across and holds her face in both hands:

"How did you know I wanted this? It's all the Schubert—the sonatas, the German dances."

"I didn't want to get you the Mozart—it would be like saying she can do it better."

"She can do everything better."

"I wouldn't say that."

Sophie looks down. She's thinking he hasn't brought her a present.

He reaches into his pocket and pulls out an envelope.

"I didn't know what to get you. I can't give you anything to wear."

She opens the letter slowly. It's three pages long.

"Read it later. Just look at what's inside."

A card falls on to the table. Written in careful handwriting are the words:

"I.O.U. I promise to take my one and only love to Venice in June."

Sophie's eyes fill with tears.

"But how can you?"

"I've thought about it. June is three months after the birth. Carla can take the baby to see her parents in Arezzo. I take you to Venice."

"And what about Tom? What do I tell him?"

"Say you're going to visit your sister. But tell her now, about us. You need someone to talk to."

Sophie is wiping her eyes.

"It's not the right time to go to Venice. Do you know how much they charge for a gondola ride in June?"

*

It isn't the weather or the tourists that stop them going to Venice. The events of the next few weeks put all thoughts of the promise out of Joseph's mind. Carla is feeling queasy at the thought of cooking, so somehow he has to prepare the festive meals. On Christmas Eve he arrives home with three heavy bags. As he sets the food down in the kitchen he wonders who to call for advice. He thinks of phoning Sophie; picks up his mobile but instead finds himself dialling his mother's number. He walks round the kitchen putting vegetables in the fridge and opening a cupboard to see that he has the porcini mushrooms for the risotto. His mother is explaining to him how to fry an eel for the Christmas Eve meal, and how to roast a goose.

"Mamma, we're not having goose. There's only two of us. I bought this little chicken. How do I cook it?"

He listens for half an hour to detailed instructions for the bird.

" ... and remember you need pancetta and onion and celery and garlic for the goose risotto for the next day."

"Mamma" he interrupts, "I told you we're not having goose."

"It doesn't matter, you need the same things and you can do it with chicken."

There never is a goose risotto, or even a chicken one. On December 26th Carla begins to feel ill and after days of pain and vomiting she is finally taken into hospital.

CHAPTER 25

Sophie knows nothing of this. She hasn't seen Joseph for a week or so. Their furtive meetings in London have been weighed down with sadness. They never seem to laugh any more, but talk over coffee, with their eyes darting about, fearful of being seen. He tells her about his concerts and the pieces he's playing. She seems preoccupied, with none of the joy that used to come tumbling out whenever they were together. There is one subject which is never mentioned.

On Christmas day he sends her a text message:

"Buon Natale. I love you."

She doesn't respond. A tear has fallen on her phone. She wipes it away with her sleeve.

They are preparing to go to Gemma for Christmas day. The car is filled with expensive gifts and Tom is hurrying her out of the door. She is wondering how she will get through hours of watching the children open their presents, fretting over toys that have no batteries or squealing over dolls that cry and pee at the press of a button.

Her sister isn't the greatest cook and will be having difficulty producing the festive meal. Her normal repertoire is limited to chicken nuggets or fish fingers at 6pm. An hour later when the children are in bed, the exhausted parents often sit down to a pile of overcooked spaghetti with the contents of a jar of pesto sliding over the top.

The task of serving up a golden turkey with the requisite trimmings is daunting. The Christmas countdowns explained in magazines take no account of the difficulties: a huge bird may not fit in a small oven; it's hard to get the legs cooked without overcooking the breast. Gemma is struggling with a large tin of potatoes that won't roast, stuffing that's oozing out, and vegetables that have been boiling away, forgotten, till they are soggy and pale. Her husband isn't around to watch the children. He's looking for the carving knife. When the turkey is finally brought to the table, with everyone mercifully hungry at the late timing—nearly 3pm—Tom swallows a mouthful of overcooked white meat and mutters something appreciative.

Sophie is dreading the three drinks parties of the next few days; she'll need heavy make-up to disguise the tautness in her face. But however hard she tries she can't conceal from Tom the heaviness in her heart. They pass each other when she goes towards the wardrobe, searching for an appropriate outfit, while he checks that the towels are straight in the bathroom. He assumes that her sombre mood is all about the usual question of children; he has no idea that Sophie's misery is caused by the impending birth of Joseph's baby.

There are three more messages from Joseph on Sophie's phone. He cannot know that she has played his words over and over again. Her fingers are wet from tears as she presses the replay button, imagining him stubbing out his cigarette and shaking his head in bewilderment as he walks back into his house.

part three

AFTER

Chapter 26

All four parents had flown in from Italy for Carla's funeral. Joseph found them rooms in a nearby street, telling them it was only somewhere to sleep. They filled the flat with their presence. If they'd been in Arezzo the body would have been laid out in a coffin in the room that was kept for best, the neighbours filing in, bearing pastries; close friends arriving with more food for the mourning family. In South London the two mothers began the day with an argument over who was going to cook the pasta. Joseph needed to speak to the undertaker. When he put down the phone they were quarrelling over the relative merits of ribollita or acquacotta. When they finally sat down at the table there was a silence, broken by the slurping of the soup and the odd comment that the vegetables in Kennington bore no resemblance to vegetables in Tuscany. Joseph kept jumping up to see to another detail of the burial and in the end the food was barely touched and the two mothers cleared the table with a noisy clattering of spoons and forks.

Two days later Joseph stood side by side with his father-in-law in the graveyard of the Catholic church in Camberwell. No mention was made of the ill feeling between them. Not a word was spoken about the extraordinary behaviour at the wedding or the unspeakable name Carla's father used to describe his son-in-law. Joseph wondered whether he'd been wrong; taking Carla to England with no thought for her elderly parents. He kept his eyes straight ahead as the coffin was lowered into the grave. He didn't see the grief or hear the sobbing. The old man turned away and walked up the path, following the women.

They were all due to return to Italy in the late afternoon. In those few hours they managed to find a final cause for argument. At the hospital the men stood uncertainly at the entrance to the Special Care Baby Unit. They were allowed in, two at a time. Joseph's mother wanted to hold the baby and whispered tenderly 'poverino, ma com'e gracilino'; Carla's mother seemed too nervous to take him out of the incubator and referred to him as 'un soldo di cacio'—a poor little scrap. What would Carla herself have made of it all? Did she even know she'd had a baby? That he'd slipped out through a film of unconsciousness?

Joseph left them at the airport and made his way back by tube. At the station a cold wind whistled through the telephone boxes, whisking the advertising cards on to the ground. Inside the flat was the accumulated mess of a week of visitors. Joseph made no effort to clear it up and walked straight over to the piano. His hands were so cold he could hardly separate the sheets of music. He was working on Beethoven's sonata No 7 and began to go over the largo, with its sad, ponderous opening. He had been confident about the rhythmic marching of the left hand, but now with his fingers frozen he was struggling with the trills and scales of the right hand. It was tempting to play too fast, creating an aggressive fog; he needed to keep control of the sustain pedal to achieve a fluid performance. The melody seemed to take flight and then collapse again. It was clearly composed by a man who was deeply depressed, reflecting fits of temper and passion, but this only hammered into his head the reminder of his own melancholy state of mind.

He remembered a teacher in his after-school music lesson telling him about Beethoven. The composer had apparently said:

"He who understands my music will be free of the suffering of the world."

Joseph was fourteen and knew nothing of suffering, least of all that of a deaf composer. At the time he'd been impatient, wanting to get on with playing the piece, so he could finally go home after a long day. But although he couldn't understand what the teacher had said, he was going through his own period of teenage anxiety. On Saturdays he walked with his friends, looking for girls, keen to find one who would go dancing with him. Some of his mates had a scooter, which made it easier. They'd see a pretty girl, drive past and drop a note at her feet. The wording was always the same: 'se vuoi venire sul mio scooter, fammelo sapere — (if you want a ride on my scooter, let me know.)'

If the girl said yes, they'd drive to an open square on the outskirts of the town, set up a CD player and blast out the latest pop music. One evening Joseph found himself on the back seat of a friend's car, with a Swedish girl he'd met in a cafe. Things were going well on the way to the square and the two couples had the space to themselves, dancing to the music of Whitney Houston and Take That. He felt the girl shiver as he mouthed the words to 'I will always love you'. In the car on the way back, he continued to hum 'Why can't I wake up with you?' as he tried to discover what was underneath a summer skirt. The girl slapped his face and left him with a red mark and a humiliation that stayed with him for weeks.

*

Joseph shook his head and put his hands on the keys. He realised he was far from understanding the Beethoven; playing it served only as a temporary block for his own misery. But forcing himself to get back to the piano was certainly better than the paralysing inactivity he'd felt in the days before the funeral.

A knock on the door broke into Joseph's thoughts. It was probably his neighbour, Mrs. Charles, complaining about the music. She used to do it in the nicest possible way, asking if he could play a little quieter:

"It's me headaches, dear. Any noise and it gets me going."

He stopped playing and went to open the door, glancing round at the state of the room. He was wrong. This time she hadn't come to complain.

"Mr. Maggiore, I brought you something."

She was holding a casserole, covered with a chequered cloth. She looked for a space on the table and Joseph cleared away a pile of papers, a shirt and some unopened letters.

"It's Lancashire hotpot, dear, with the dumplings."

"Dumplings? What is that?"

Mrs. Charles told him what they were and he was finding it hard to imagine little lumps of dough like gnocchi floating in a meat stew. He wondered what the food would be like. He and Carla used to joke about what the English ate: a roast with no garlic, lamb without rosmarino. Worst of all were the salads, drenched in balsamic vinegar with hardly a trace of olive oil.

"How's the baby?"

Mrs. Charles was fiddling with the buttons of her coat. He knew she was avoiding the subject of Carla's death.

"So, so—he is better, he is worse."

"I've heard you playing the piano more. You seem to be in most of the time."

"Yes, I am."

He wished she would go away. Did she know that he hadn't been to the hospital for days? In the mornings he forced himself to go out for milk and bread and then came back and practised for a few hours. By mid-afternoon he was drained and slumped into a chair and slept. He woke up with a stiff neck and could only rouse himself again at the thought of a drink. Most evenings he threw on a jacket and scarf and walked round to the off-licence for a bottle of wine.

"When's the baby coming home? I can help you if you like—to get ready and that. The place could do with a bit of a clear up."

Joseph looked at her face. In spite of the wrinkles she had the sweet smile of a young girl. He squeezed her arm and thanked her. When she had gone he went back to the sonata, but decided to abandon the largo and work on the melodic third movement. The beginning was as simple as a piece written for a child, but while the left hand kept a slow rhythm the right played dancing trills which made his fingers ache. The insistent repeat of three notes leading to a series of scales needed endless practice. It took all his strength to play it through once, but he needed to build up his stamina. Having stopped numerous times he began the whole piece from the beginning and then, without a pause, started to play it a second time. If he could play it through twice, he'd have no difficulty when it came to the concert.

Carla was never out of his mind. He should have done something about her depression. She'd almost stopped cooking but in spite of that she seemed to be putting on weight. Perhaps she ate during the evenings when he was out, filling herself with chocolate or slices of salami? He'd misread the most obvious signs: biscuit wrappers and empty crisp packets stuffed behind the toaster. Instead of berating her for never clearing up, he should have helped.

Did anyone ever suggest that Beethoven should see someone to treat his melancholy? No, of course not, there weren't any therapists in those days. But in his case he should have taken Carla to the doctor, asked why she had no energy; explored the reason for her apparent misery, or at least got some medication to make it bearable. Perhaps she should have spent more time with her family? The idea of staying with her parents appealed to her, but she was nervous of travelling alone, needing Joseph by her side to deal with the fear of the unfamiliar.

The memory of the time in June when he took her to Italy was so vivid and shocking that he tried to put it out of his mind. It was easier to rerun the uncomplicated events; the day-to-day nonsense conversations. But in almost every waking moment— apart from when he was at the piano—the thoughts kept coming back. They were like well-thumbed photographs, dusted, polished and fingered but still refusing to fade. He could turn them on, like a slide show, pausing and forwarding to the bits he wanted to dwell on, gliding over the parts that caused him pain.

CHAPTER 27

Tom went over the conversation he'd had with the policeman. How dare he ask if his wife had been happy. He'd responded to that ridiculous question with an outburst about the driver of the car:

"Of course Sophie was happy. And she'd still be here now if this idiot hadn't killed her."

The policeman was young and had little experience of dealing with bereavement. The conversation couldn't have taken a worse turn. He told Tom that the driver was so devastated that he hadn't been able to go back to work.

Tom closed the front door, relieved that the questions were over. The heavy boots had left a mark on the pale carpet. It was too soon for him to have any thoughts for the driver of the car; to think how he must have felt when he rushed up to Sophie's still body; to wonder whether he got back in the car to continue his journey; to imagine what he did in the following days. Tom had no idea that this man was also waking up with his pyjamas damp from sweat, unable to face the morning light.

The clock was showing ten thirty in the morning. The minute-hand seemed to be going slower, as if it were clogged with grease.

The mechanism was clearly working but it seemed to him as if time had slowed down ever since the moment when he heard the news. Each hour had acquired extra minutes so a day with nothing to look forward to stretched out to an interminable length. His task was simply to get through the hours of daylight. Then as evening crept in, it brought with it a different silence, hours without Sophie telling him what she'd been up to, what she'd bought that day. The chatter of television continued well after midnight, ushering in a restless night of black thoughts. When dawn came it signalled the start of another bleak day.

Each morning brought a new problem: not on the scale of a major, world-shattering incident, but enough to make him feel constantly unsettled. It was as if the force of Sophie's death had whipped through his life like a hurricane, leaving a trickle of day-to-day irritations. Inconsequential things blew up out of all proportion. He had no clean shirts. Sophie had taken them to be laundered and he had no idea where the shop was. He'd tried to clean the lavatory and poured bleach into the bowl, splashing his jeans and finding later they were dotted with permanent white specks. There was a rancid smell all through the flat. Dead flowers sat in stagnant, murky water and the rubbish bin in the kitchen was overflowing—filled with reeking melon skins and the whiff of stale fish from an empty pack of salmon fillets. Trying to change the bed linen he discovered that you need four hands to put on a duvet cover. Even a simple meal like steak and onions had proved impossible. No-one had told him that vegetables go limp if you start cooking them in cold oil. By the time the pan was sizzling, the smoke alarm was shrieking through the flat. Tom reached for the grill pan, removed the charred steak and burned his wrist as he flung the rack and the pan into the sink. Two days later it was still there, blocking the plughole as droplets of grease floated on top of the cold water from the tap.

The day of the funeral had come and gone. There must have been conversations with undertakers and decisions to make about music and flowers. His mind was a blur of flight arrival times and certificates. Someone had to meet his sister-in-law from New York and five separate documents needed to be signed for the cremation. He had a faint memory of sitting at his computer and finding a website called 'ifish' It turned out that the full name was 'ifishoulddie.com'. Tom reflected that the name was wrong because if he should die, he wouldn't need all the information it offered. He scrolled through the pages, ignoring the comment that pacemakers explode in high temperatures. He printed out some of the more useful advice: the reminder to return Sophie's library books and the fact that filled teeth had to be removed before a body was cremated.

The eulogy read by Sophie's father referred to her loving nature and generosity, but Tom could only think about the empty space in his bed. While her sisters talked about the little presents she'd bought for them, his thoughts were focused on the breasts he'd never touch again; the feeling of moving his finger between her legs.

After the service they all came back to the flat and the pale room was filled with children climbing over the furniture, wiping sticky fingers on the dining chairs. Tom had ordered a platter of Middle Eastern pastries from The Orient and flakes of syrupy filo were now embedded in the corners of the sofa. Eventually the adults got up to leave. Gemma was taking her father and sister to stay with her. Debs brushed Tom's cheek with a kiss and mumbled 'anything I can do, just call.' At last he could breathe again. Alone in his pastel space he tried to obliterate the past week from his mind.

The time spent with Sophie's family after the funeral had left him feeling edgy. Regret and recriminations poured into his head. Tom wondered when it was that the eccentric clothes buying changed from a subject of amusement to one of irritation. Perhaps he should have seen that Sophie was a fragile bird, not a simple shopaholic?

He picked up his filofax and realised that he hadn't yet inserted the diary section for the new year. He began to turn over the pages, leafing back through the months, trying to hold on to the life they had before. In his mind events were now classified as pre January 3rd and post January 3rd. Nothing after that date had any significance. Events before then were bathed in a glow which he called happiness.

CHAPTER 28

Women write thoughts in their diaries. Men make brief notes of times and meetings. The entries in his Filofax welcomed Tom into the past and obliterated the post-January misery. He lay down on the bed and closed his eyes, going over their life together before that speeding car brought it all to an end.

For weeks he'd been keeping his appointments and trying to stay outwardly calm. When someone muttered words of sympathy, he replied brusquely, wishing they hadn't referred to Sophie. As long as his mind was filled with work and the discussions were about paintings he could behave normally. As soon as someone mentioned the accident or reminded him of Sophie's kindnesses, he felt the tears pricking behind his eyes.

At times he thought he was getting over it. Their friends would phone up and invite him for dinner. The conversation would be going fine, then someone would say something, quite unintentionally, that would blow a frosty silence across the table.

It was usually an innocent comment: 'Are you still travelling, Tom? It must be fun going to all those new places.'

When he replied that travelling alone—even on business—wasn't much fun, no-one seemed to know what to say. The invitations gradually dried up and his friends no longer included him, crossing his name out of their mental table plans. It was as if a single presence threatened the stability of their lives as couples.

Yet there was no shortage of people to do things with. The names of artists and hotel managers filled his address book. What he missed was someone to do nothing with. Breakfast with Sophie had often been almost silent, but she had been there, sitting opposite him, grunting at the butter that was too hard to spread; tut tutting at a piece of news in the paper. Now there was no-one there to say 'pass the milk', no-one to tell him his breath wasn't as fresh as it could be, handing him a stick of chewing gum as he went out of the door. Friends he hadn't seen for months suddenly appeared on the doorstep, hugging him but unable to say any words of comfort. Many brought chocolates. He had nine boxes piled up in a cupboard. The fresh cream ones were well past their best and the dark mints were of the kind that never go off, being handed from one weight-watcher to another. Tom had never liked chocolates. His weakness was something that Sophie would never cook: a fry-up. He remembered her complaining:

"You're not serious. How can you eat all that butter?"

"Easy, I'll show you."

Tom had never pretended he had any skills in the kitchen, but he had learned about the fry-up at school. The senior boys were allowed to cook and the dream meal he'd perfected was a towering pile of bread fried in butter, topped with eggs scrambled in butter. Baked beans and a sliced banana were heated in more butter and poured over the top. Assembling it all needed no skill, but great speed.

Now for some reason he couldn't bring himself to make the fry-up. When he was working he concluded deals over restaurant food, elaborately arranged on large square plates. His favourite orders were mussels or a neat little rack of lamb and his only regret was that he couldn't suck the meat off the bones, as he might have done at home. But this never happened since his repertoire didn't include any fancy dishes. It was limited to a bacon sandwich or a plate of cornflakes. So Tom poured himself yet another bowl of cereal, filling it up with milk and pressing down the flakes with his fingers, till they were all submerged.

He sat down to watch the news on television. The newsreader announced the headlines and the picture changed to the main story of the day. At five past six, Tom had finished his supper. He took the empty bowl back into the kitchen and for the first time that day, felt the beginning of a smile. At least there was no wafting odour of broccoli in the flat. That was one of the foul-smelling green vegetables that Sophie used to cook.

CHAPTER 29

Two months after Sophie's death, Tom was opening his post with a glass-handled paperknife. It was the last birthday present she'd given him. He piled up the envelopes and began to read the letters. The first one was from the police:

"March 4th

Reference SF 31

Dear Mr. Fielding,

We have to inform you that we shall not be pursuing a prosecution in connection with the accident that involved your wife. Please don't hesitate in contacting us if you wish to discuss the matter further.

Yours etc."

He threw the letter aside and began to deal with his other correspondence. One of his artists had failed to produce the volume of paintings needed for a hotel in Nice.

'Accident' he thought; 'it wasn't an accident'.

There was another problem in Vienna. He'd ordered sixty charcoal drawings and when the consignment was unpacked a dozen of the frames were found to contain cracked glass. He had barely two weeks to get the pictures reframed.

'Involved your wife'—what did that mean? She had been killed. Tom tried to distract himself by concentrating on the other letters. He underlined the phone numbers in Nice and Vienna. But his fingers started to dial the local police station.

What did they mean when they said they 'don't have enough evidence?'

The call was redirected to another number. When he finally got through an unfamiliar police officer answered his questions.

"Mr. Fielding, I believe my colleague has been through this before. There's no way we can prosecute without a witness."

"But you've got two people who saw it."

"They don't support your belief that the driver was speeding."

"But he was clearly driving dangerously."

"Not necessarily. Let me put it like this. For us to build a case we have to prove that the motorist was either speeding or drunk. We've eliminated the second possibility because he was breathalysed at the scene. If we try to prove the first we need witnesses who will say he was driving over the speed limit."

The policeman seemed to be saying that the driver may not have been responsible for the death, even though he was driving the car that caused it.

"Are you saying that the witnesses will say it was Sophie's fault?"

"That wasn't what I was going to say. Mr. Fielding, an accident can have many causes. By the very nature of the word 'accident', it could just be something that happened—with no-one to blame. And then again, it's possible that the driver was faced with something beyond his control."

"I don't know what you're saying. He was in control of the car. He has to accept responsibility for what happened."

"As you wish, Sir. But as I say, our decision stays the same."

Tom put the phone down and returned to his work. He was so depressed he could think of nothing but worries. A consignment of abstract designs for Amsterdam proved to be too heavy to hang above the hotel beds. The internal walls were so flimsy that the framed pictures were in danger of falling down, possibly even injuring a hotel guest. Then, at another hotel, some small works by a German artist called Kuhn were disappearing from the walls for another reason. They were stylish interpretations of Mondrian, Calder and Miro, each with a miniature figure perching on a line or block of colour. The paintings were small enough to fit in a suitcase and some of the hotel guests were taking them home as souvenirs.

For once Tom began to regret that he was self-employed. If he'd worked in an office he could have delegated some of these problems or shared his concerns with a colleague. Now he had no-one to speak to. He could hardly reveal to his friends that work was not going well. It never occurred to him to pick up the phone to Sophie's sisters, so there was one option left—to speak to his mother in Spain.

"Hi Mum, how's the bridge going?"

Caroline seemed taken aback at the surprise phone call, but quickly recovered and launched into a description of one of the hands the night before:

"Peter was my partner. He opened One Spade and I had nineteen points and four spades to the King Jack. So I bid Six Spades. Peter's spades were four to the ten nine. He messed up the play and went down four vulnerable. That was eleven hundred. I don't know why I play with him."

"Wow" said Tom.

In the silence he could hear the tinkle of ice in a glass. He wanted to talk to his mother about trying to cope with Sophie's sudden death. The conversation—if that's what it could be called—continued for another half an hour, with Caroline telling him details of menus in the local restaurant and gossip about fellow ex-pats he'd never heard of.

This time it wasn't his mother who put the phone down first. Tom brought the call to a close, having revealed nothing of his state of mind. At the beginning of the next bridge game Caroline smiled and told her partner that she'd had a 'lovely chat' with her son.

"He's so busy, poor lamb. It's so good of him to find the time to speak to his mother and find out what's going on in her life."

CHAPTER 30

"Joseph, where the hell are you? It's Richard. I need to talk to you."

He'd left three messages and there was no response. After that embarrassing time with Carla, and the discovery that Joseph was doing something suspicious on his trips abroad, there had been little contact between them for months. Joseph had probably told his wife he didn't need anyone to represent him but it was obvious to Richard that the diary was empty. It needed time and effort to go out and secure the bookings. How could Joseph devote time to anything other than practice and play?

When Richard and Joseph made contact again, it was on the same impersonal level as before. There was no friendship between the agent and the artist, and certainly little interest on either side about the details of their lives.

For a man who managed others, Richard was surprisingly insensitive. He had no knowledge of music or of the concentration needed to perform in public. Performers were his clients. He didn't try to understand them or their concerns. He never discussed with Joseph what he was doing in Europe on his fake engagements. He simply took him on again and entered dates in his diary.

After Carla became ill he didn't hear from Joseph for a few weeks. With the shocking news of her death, he thought it best to keep his distance. In the weeks that followed he preferred to put her whole existence out of his mind. He was not the kind of man who would think about a husband's loss and try it on for size.

*

Joseph glared at the flashing light and deleted the messages on the machine. He went back to the piano and continued with the Beethoven sonata. The challenging dialogue between the two hands was beginning to come together but he still had the apprehension of playing a piece in public for the first time. The date of the lunchtime concert at St. John Smith Square was looming closer. At least this one would pay a few bills.

Just after he'd won the prize, as a student of twenty two, he'd played at free concerts and was happy to have a booking at the Blackheath Halls, even if there was no fee. But this one was different; a more demanding audience, settling into packed rows downstairs, with a few leaning over from the upstairs gallery.

The nerves would start the afternoon before—the queasiness in the stomach, the dry mouth, and just before the performance he'd have to force himself to eat something. He once gobbled a whole bar of chocolate minutes before a concert and found himself desperately thirsty ten minutes later. Since then he always chose a banana. It reminded him of his first competition. A dozen players were waiting their turn, pacing the room. He was the last to play and watched from the side as each pianist went on. Finally it was time for him to walk on to the stage. His hands were damp as he clasped the score. He took out a tissue to wipe his fingers and aimed it at a bin. He had no idea then why the bin was filled with banana skins.

There was no point phoning Richard—he just needed to get the allegro right. He'd mastered the melodic repetition moving from the left to the right hand; he had done exercises to improve his hand span; but he was still having difficulty with the rapid fingering at the end of the movement. It was hard enough having to think about whether he'd be able to perform, without having to contend with Richard. He could see him now, poking at his palm pilot with its little stylus, wanting to go over the arrangements in his meticulous way. Joseph remembered being irritated by a discussion on the subject of an encore. Richard had asked him if he'd thought of one and received a snappy reply in response:

"No, of course not: there's no need. It's a lunchtime concert, people have to get back to work."

Joseph hadn't bothered to tell Richard that you don't 'think' of an encore. Professionals have a repertoire of a dozen extra pieces. They don't need to practise them in advance; they can judge from the strength of the audience applause how many to do. The most important thing is not to rush off the stage immediately. It's even best to stand there for a full ten seconds before taking the first bow. The audience will rarely stop clapping as long as the pianist is still on the stage.

The doorbell rang and there was Richard, wearing the checked shirt and yellow bow-tie that he thought made him look artistic. He glanced round the room.

"I see you've tidied up."

"Not me. it's my neighbour Mrs. Charles. Sh ... she's in the kitchen."

He didn't tell Richard that she'd told him he had to 'bring himself together' or something like that.

"Joseph. We need to talk about your next booking. How's it going for the lunchtime concert?"

"Don't ask. The Beethoven's coming along but I have to work on the Bach."

"Do you know it yet?"

"What do you think?"

Richard had no idea of what it took to learn a piece. It wasn't simply a matter of mastering the notes—more like making sense of the melody, the phrase structure. It was like peeling an onion, moving on to the next level, working on the harmonies and the climaxes and the contrasting sections.

Joseph's thoughts were interrupted by Mrs. Charles. She came out of the kitchen and asked:

"I'm doing the fridge. What do you want with cheese that's goin' orf and this raw looking meat?"

"Prosciutto, Mrs. Charles. It's ham. The best, from Parma."

"I don't care what it is dear, it doesn't smell good to me. Chuck it out, with all these rotten vegetables."

She then moved on and started scrubbing away at the stains in the washbasin. The week before she'd tackled the bedroom. It was when she'd finished hoovering the carpet that she gave her opinion on another matter and suggested that Joseph should get rid of Carla's clothes.

"She said what?" asked Richard, when Joseph repeated the conversation to him.

"She persuaded me. She said something like 'you can't be doin' with 'avin' 'er things around.'"

"Why do you take any notice of her? She's not exactly a bright spark, is she?"

Joseph didn't reply.

"Anyway, what did you do with them?" asked Richard.

"Put them in the bags, for the bin."

"You didn't."

"What was I supposed to do? Send them to Arezzo to her parents? Whatever I do with the clothes, for her father, is my fault. He already thinks I'm a monster. Do I have to ask them what I should do with every skirt, every pair of shoes?"

"Hey, chill out. I just thought. you shouldn't have been so hasty."

Joseph muttered something in Italian and continued to justify his actions.

"It's been twenty days. Twenty days of looking at her clothes, hearing her high heels click click on the floors, you don't understand. Richard, I'm sorry, I need to practise."

He flicked back a page of the sonata and began the slow repetitive tune of the allegro, speeding up to the quick finger movements with the right hand. He was trying to get back to the way he played before Carla's depression. Perhaps, subconsciously, he had stopped and repeated phrases more than he needed? Perhaps he was trying to be annoying? It was one thing immersing himself in scales but quite another to keep beginning the difficult bars again and again, trying to perfect the fingering. When he pressed the playback button on the mini disc player, he could have used headphones, instead of blasting his imperfect performance all through the flat.

He remembered a conversation he'd had with Sophie, when she'd suggested he had been unsympathetic:

"Maybe you're a bit hard on Carla. She has to listen to the endless repetition—as it seems to her—and yet she never gets to hear you play the finished piece at a concert."

"But that's her choice" he'd replied.

"Maybe. But she's missing out. It's like a girlfriend standing by the side of a football pitch in the cold and rain, watching a training session. Everyone knows it's more fun to catch the highlights of a big match on the news in the evening. That way you just get to see the goals and hear the cheering."

Joseph was flattered that Sophie had likened his concerts to a game watched by millions. But the smile quickly vanished and his mouth was like a knife blade as he blamed himself, yet again, for Carla's sad view of their life together.

*

Richard must have let himself out. Joseph felt a further twinge of guilt, thinking that he hadn't been exactly polite. But now that he'd confronted his behaviour with his wife, he reproached himself even more as he remembered how his repetitive playing had caused the row with Carla; how one day—over a year ago—he'd been preparing for another lunchtime concert and he'd slammed down the piano lid and walked out of the flat.

CHAPTER 31

Mrs. Charles must have left. Joseph was alone in the flat. He played the Beethoven without stopping in an effort to banish the thoughts in his head. He looked at his watch and pulled on his jacket, checking to see that he had the mobile and keys in his pocket. He closed the front door and wondered for the hundredth time, whether he should try to contact Sophie.

"No, it's finished." he thought. "What's the point of starting it again, with all that waiting, all the pain?"

In the weeks before Carla's illness he'd reached for his phone so many times. It was only when his wife was in hospital that he'd stopped. He'd been so tempted to tell Sophie what had happened but the days had passed, and after Matteo's birth there had seemed no point. The intensity of their meetings, the passion they had shared—all this seemed so far away from reality. His wife was dead and he was alone with a child who was struggling for his life. Nothing Sophie could say would be of any help.

She'd calmed him down before a concert and reassured him that they weren't doing any harm to anyone, but she would have no understanding of the turbulence in his mind. He could hardly explain it to himself: the joy of holding the baby, feeling the breath in his body, the warmth; the urge to stroke his eyebrows, run his finger over the tiny mouth and feel Matteo's fingers close around his own. And then ... the terror he felt at the thought of losing him.

He arrived at the hospital and ran along the corridor past the wool tapestries on the wall. Instead of taking the clanking lift he climbed the stone stairs and then slowed down for the last flight of metal rimmed steps. He pressed the buzzer and went into the room. He stood panting for a few minutes and then realised that Matteo wasn't in his incubator. A feeling of panic spread a bright colour up his throat but before he could speak a nurse came over to him:

"Joseph. He's been moved. He's in the next room."

"Why? what does it mean?"

"Don't worry. It's good news. The room he's in now is cooler. He can maintain his body heat better and doesn't need the higher temperature in here."

A week before Matteo had contracted a further infection. Four or five other babies in the unit were suffering like him. All Joseph remembered were snatches of conversations with the doctors: 'Possible heart murmur', 'heart valve open'. But the infection had receded and now his baby had been moved to a less dependent area, known to some of the parents as The Senior School. Joseph put into words the thought that came to him every time he looked at the weight chart, increasing every day by a tiny amount: 30g— about an ounce.

"So, he's going to be all right?"

Nurses and doctors were faced with this question every day. There was no answer even for a normal size baby. Who knows what might happen next week, in a year or two, or in twenty? To survive, a premature baby needs to be on a path where tomorrow has to be better than today. Joseph worded the question another way:

"So, he's out of danger?"

The nurse could see how Joseph was trying to turn it into a statement, willing it to be true. She did her best to respond.

"All right? We can't say. We're monitoring his feeding carefully because of the infection. Every few days we take a few drops of blood from his heel. He may need a transfusion tomorrow, to top him up again."

She didn't comment that Joseph hadn't been for days. The staff were used to parents who came twice a day, then for some reason couldn't face it and weren't seen for a week. In the next room Joseph asked the nurse if he could hold Matteo. He opened the two doors of the incubator, disconnected the wires and lifted the baby out with one hand. He looked down at Matteo's translucent skin and saw that the little chest rising and falling was no wider than the breadth of his own hand. Suddenly the baby gave a little jump and then seemed still.

"What's happening? Did he stop breathing?"

"No," said the nurse. "But I have to tell you he stopped three times last night."

"O dio. How is this possible? His brain—without breathing it must be damage."

Joseph's English always got worse when he was nervous. The nurse continued talking:

"There's no danger as long as it's for less than fifteen seconds. When we hear the alarm we come and flick his foot. There's always one of us who can reach the incubator in that time. Remember, we're in training."

Joseph couldn't manage a smile, but he looked relieved.

"I ... I think he's getting cold. Shall we put him back?"

He opened the two round doors and gently laid the baby in the incubator. He couldn't get out of his mind the possibility that one day he'd arrive to find Matteo still, not breathing. With Carla's death he was mourning a past life: how they'd grown into adulthood together, learned to manage in a strange city. Her loss had left him with regrets for the present and memories of the years they'd shared. But if Matteo were to die, there would only be a handful of things to remember: the touch of his skin, the smell of his hair, the warmth of his fragile body. The baby's whole future could be snuffed out in a second. He would never take his first tentative steps, or walk into his first day at primary school. There would be no brief parting as the boy left to begin a student life, no calls from university. If Matteo ceased to exist, Joseph would never know what path he might have taken. Would he have been a sportsman, a scientist, a shopkeeper? Would he have settled down with a plump Italian girl or a dark-skinned woman from Asia; a Catholic or a Hindu; a home-maker or a high-flyer in the world of banking?

His thoughts were interrupted by the nurse:

"I think you should start feeding him. You've seen us do it enough times. Watch me now and then you can do it yourself tomorrow."

She wrapped the baby firmly in an extra blanket and went to get a syringe.

"Look, first you attach it to the tube in his nose, then you need to hold it above his head. Squeeze it very gently and then it'll start to flow on its own. It's easy. This amount takes ten minutes or so. It's about a spoonful of milk. It's not a pint of Guinness."

The last drops of milk were draining through the syringe. Another nurse was walking round the room, stopping at each incubator.

"Joseph this is Katarina. She's in charge of neonatal development."

He found it hard to follow her Swedish accent. She was saying something about the light in the room affecting babies' brains. Joseph had no idea what she was talking about. He didn't want to know about possible outcomes. He'd already imagined that perhaps Matteo might be deaf. Did anyone else notice that he never turned his head at a sudden loud noise? He kept this particular worry to himself, for fear of seeming over anxious. Katarina was still speaking. Joseph's only thought was how to extricate himself. What came out was rather abrupt:

"Good to meet you. I have to go."

He started to walk away but she followed him, talking rapidly in a low voice:

"You see, it's all about keeping the stress levels down."

Joseph could feel his own stress level rising. When he was sitting at the piano, his mind kept wandering to Matteo, curled up on his side with probes attached to his finger and his head. At the hospital, Joseph's thoughts turned to the music he should be playing.

Presented with the reality of the baby's situation, and his inability to do anything other than watch what the professionals were doing, Joseph switched off and began to think about a particular passage in the Bach partita. The opening needed to be crisp and driving. His mood was anything but brisk, so to settle his nerves he made himself picture the score in front of his eyes, mentally turning the pages. He found his fingers subconsciously moving in slow triple time.

"As I was saying. we keep the lights down and the incubators are covered with blankets."

All Joseph could think about was the music. He couldn't wait to get back to the piano to practise the ascending passages and master the repeats of the melody. He edged out of the room, leaving the woman still talking.

CHAPTER 32

Joseph didn't expect to meet anyone he knew at St. Mary's. Since he'd started to feed Matteo, he was at the hospital every day. Apart from Mrs. Charles the neighbours were unaware of what had happened. He had a number of acquaintances in the music business but they hardly even knew of the baby's existence.

In Arezzo no-one would speak of a pregnancy before the third month. It would be tempting the evil-eye, the malocchio. When Carla had reached the fourth and fifth month her condition had not yet become obvious because she didn't approve of the tight fitting clothes other pregnant women wore. She refused to reveal inches of bare flesh between a stretched t-shirt and a pair of low slung trousers. She concealed her bulge so well that their friends saw nothing but her usual rounded figure. When she died, it came as a shock to everyone who knew them. At the funeral people murmured about 'diabetic complications', 'pancreatitis' and a tiny premature baby. In the weeks that followed, they were too nervous to make contact and many of them assumed that the baby hadn't survived.

Richard was different. He knew why Joseph had practically stopped working and often asked after Matteo, but his questions seemed perfunctory. So it came as a surprise when one day in March, Joseph encountered him at the hospital.

"What are you doing here?"

"They told me there are no fixed visiting times." He was wondering if he should have brought a bunch of grapes. Not knowing what to say he carried on talking:

"I thought I might find you here. You never answer the phone. We need to talk."

They walked together into the unit. Richard said little as they stood by the incubator.

"His head looks a bit flat."

"It could be much worse."

Joseph's economy of words often extended outside the environment of his piano playing. He didn't think it worth explaining what happens to the skull if a baby doesn't move much. The flattening occurs because the bones of premature babies are soft and they lie first on one side and are then turned over to the other.

"Aren't you worried about it, it looks a bit squashed?"

"I'm worried about a thousand things. But you don't see many people walking around with flattened heads, so I assume it'll make itself right."

"He looks so fragile" said Richard.

"He's more tough than you think. He won't break. Do you want to hold him?"

Joseph looked at Richard's face, perfectly shaven, with the thin mouth wavering slightly at the thought of putting out an immaculate cuffed shirtsleeve. He looked down at his own crumpled clothes and seemed aware for the first time that he no longer presented an image of a performer who was neatly dressed and confident. Anyone watching would have found them an unlikely pair: the one dark skinned and sallow, gazing at the baby; the other, standing a head taller, with his eyes darting round the room, as if to find a way of escape.

Richard didn't respond to the offer to hold the baby. A doctor had interrupted their conversation and was explaining to Joseph that Matteo would need another blood transfusion. From the first day they had been taking minute amounts of blood to test for irregularities like anaemia. It was also the simplest way to detect an infection that required treatment with antibiotics. After several of these tests, the blood needed to be replaced by a transfusion.

Joseph was listening but not taking in the words. It wasn't just a language problem: one part of his brain dealt with translation but another part sent messages to his body in moments of panic. His hand began to shake at the thought of replacing lost blood. This is what they did to adults who were in serious danger. It made no difference that the amount Matteo would need was minute; Joseph imagined valves and tubes lacking the blood that was needed to keep the heart pumping.

Richard could see it wasn't the moment to talk about future bookings. He was concerned that Joseph had a group of concerts planned for March and an empty diary after that. They needed to sit down together and have a proper discussion. Joseph was hardly working at all. He may have been adding to his repertoire but it wasn't enough to fill a major concert programme. Richard turned to have another look at Matteo. He seemed to be breathing steadily. It was lucky he hadn't brought grapes. There didn't seem to be a fruit bowl at the side of the cot.

*

The March bookings had been in the diary long before the baby's arrival. With Matteo's extended stay in hospital – and no immediate prospect of his coming home – Joseph prepared for the first concert, in Birmingham. Ever since Carla's death the performance nerves were getting worse. He carried two handkerchiefs to counteract the cold, wet hands and had taken to biting his lips to stop them quivering. At the Symphony Hall there were practice rooms for performers so after an hour at the piano, Joseph took a break and walked out on to the blond floor of the auditorium, taking in the blur of lights and the massed rows of flame-coloured seats. A fellow performer standing near him must have seen the expression on his face and guessed that his heart was pumping.

"You have to get yourself some beta blockers."

Joseph was taken aback by the man's comment:

"I thought they were for heart problems."

"They are, and that's what you've got. Your heart doesn't know why the adrenalin is racing. It could be that you're facing a tiger. On the other hand, it might just be the audience at the Symphony Hall."

"So if I take one, it'll calm me down?"

"Down from a wild panic to mild hysteria, as some famous pianist said. But you'll have to work harder."

"What do you mean? I'm already up at six."

"No, it's not about how long you practise. The drugs block the adrenalin. You just have to play better to counteract that."

Joseph now carried the pills in his pocket. After his performance at the ICC in Birmingham, he made sure he had enough packs to take to the remaining three venues. With concerts booked in Glasgow, Belfast and Stockholm he had a suit carrier and an overnight bag permanently packed, ready for the next trip. The only advantage of air travel was that he couldn't fail to get out at his destination, unlike with the train or tube when it was easy to fall asleep and miss the stop. On arrival he'd be whisked away in a taxi, hardly looking up to notice the architecture of each new city. The rain and damp seeped into his clothes, reminding him of his dislike of cold places and Carla's complaints about the eternal grey.

CHAPTER 33

Springtime in central London brought damp pavements but none of the blossoms of the suburbs. Rain always made Joseph think of that first meeting with Sophie and how it had led to a change that took him out of his passive acceptance of life, to a passion for living. Even now—months after the contact was broken—he blamed himself for the way it ended. On that day in Lisbon he knew he had caused her pain. When he'd told her it was 'for the best' he could have thought of a better lie. What could possibly be best about waking up each morning, knowing he couldn't see her, thinking about the feel of her skin, the way she looked at him?

His life with Carla was a shadow in comparison. At the beginning they'd had an easy relationship, exploring together like children, learning how to manage in a foreign country. Neither of them had been abroad before. Even their honeymoon was spent in Italy, in Argentario, seventy miles from their home town. They'd stayed at a small pensione near the sea. One day they'd gone to a resort town called Porto Ercole and wandered into a luxury hotel, with a restaurant on the beach under the shade of a white awning. The food was set out on long tables with chefs standing behind a barbecue, hovering over copper warming dishes, full of freshly grilled seafood. Joseph whispered to Carla that they should stay for lunch. She was already looking at the desserts: mountains of peaches and strawberries and almond cake dusted with sugar. Joseph went over to the head waiter and asked the price. The man flicked a finger on the lapel of his tailored jacket and replied: '22 euros'. Then he looked from one to the other, taking in the beachbag and sandals, and repeated '22 euros—each'. Joseph put his hand in his back pocket and took out his wallet. He held out a bunch of notes and said 'We'll stay.' For the rest of the week they lived on pizza.

When did it all go wrong? There was no moment when they stopped laughing and sat facing each other across a table and realised they had changed. It must have happened slowly. If they'd stayed in Arezzo it might have been different. Carla would have been more comfortable; surrounded by friends instead of being on her own in a flat in South London, bemoaning the English weather. But he'd set his sights on becoming a concert pianist. Joseph had never thought of music as the road to wealth, but he had to admit that concert fees took him to a different level of expenditure, so he could afford to buy a jacket from Zegna, instead of picking up a pair of jeans under the bright lights at Standa. In Tuscany he might have earned his living as a teacher, but having a steady job in a small town would never have been enough for him. They'd have had children, of course; maybe a boy and a girl. By the time the boy was fourteen, they'd have bought him a scooter and he'd be driving along the country roads to school. Then Carla really would have had something to worry about; but like the other parents, they'd have said nothing, waiting anxiously for the sound of his Vespa turning into their drive at the end of the school day. In the evenings, eating a meal together, he'd have snapped at the children's lazy table manners and growled at Carla about the quality of the parmesan—all because he would have had a bad day in front of a class of untalented students.

Joseph stopped thinking of what might have been and went back to playing the Bach partita. When his fingers finally rested on the keys he had a moment of satisfaction. It seemed a long time since he'd felt this confident, knowing he'd not only got the notes right but was nearer to understanding what was in the composer's mind. Years ago, when he'd entered the prize competition, the contestants had been confined for a week and set to learn a 15-minute concerto that they'd never seen before; a fiendishly difficult modern work. After his performance, when they announced he was the winner, he was in ecstasy, promising himself that nothing would ever be as hard as this. In those days he relished playing in concerts and rarely felt more than a moment's stress as he took his place on the platform. Now, with the turmoil in his personal life, panic welled up in him the moment he picked up a new score and began the weeks of practising.

Sophie had always tried to boost his confidence, telling him there was a benefit in not being on the very top rung of the professional ladder. Those performers were committed to programmes planned two to three years in advance. They had to travel to at least sixty performances a year. She reminded him of players who had memory lapses, temperamental outbursts:

"Even Andras Schiff lost it one day. He walked away from the piano in the middle of a concert because the audience wouldn't stop coughing. As he left the stage he said: 'Please use the time for further coughing.'"

Joseph had his own reason to be unsympathetic to audiences.

"Seriously, we expect something from the audience. They need to do a bit of work too. If you've never heard the music before it's harder to appreciate it. You must listen to it before you come."

Sophie thought for a moment and then said:

"I suppose it's like when you go to a dinner. The host provides the food and wine and it's up to the guest to contribute the conversation."

Joseph had no experience of dinner parties. Conversation around an Italian lunch table was noisy, fuelled by wine, littered with local gossip.

In his mind he was thinking again of the difference between his life and Sophie's. He went back to analysing the cause of the rift between him and Carla. Instead of the underlying criticism he felt in Carla's brief exchanges, there was a gentleness to Sophie's concern about his health or his work worries. She had also opened his eyes.

What began as the attraction of the unfamiliar, changed into a tender attachment—far more than just stolen days in hotel bedrooms.

Would he ever be able to stop tormenting himself about the two women he had loved? Whenever he remembered the trips abroad with Sophie, he switched to thoughts of Carla being taken to hospital. Why were the memories of her illness and death so clear and the end of his affair with Sophie so hazy? Joseph couldn't even recall the last time he had spoken to her. Now he assumed that she was rebuilding her life with Tom. In the whole sorry mess there was one good thing. Tom knew nothing.

CHAPTER 34

Joseph looked at his watch and pulled himself away from thoughts of Sophie. He had an appointment at the hospital. Since Matteo's first transfusion he'd been thinking of giving blood, so an hour later he found himself sitting in the mobile blood donor unit outside St. Mary's. He was in the queue waiting. A nurse led him to a cubicle and took a spot of blood from his finger to test for anaemia. He sat on a bench waiting his turn and after a few minutes he was led to one of the beds and told to lie down. A doctor put a cuff on his arm, pumped in air and pricked the skin to insert the needle into the vein. Immediately the blood started rushing along the tube, swelling the plastic envelope. Joseph closed his eyes and relaxed on to the couch, thinking how easy it would be to fall asleep. A nurse was sitting by his side and she asked him what he did for a living.

He wasn't in the mood for the questions that usually follow when he told people he was a concert pianist. Instead he said he was a solicitor, specialising in company law. There was no further conversation while the blood flowed silently into the envelope. When it was full, the nurse put a clamp on the tube, cut it off and squeezed three samples of blood into separate test tubes. How much would be needed to replace the blood that had been taken from Matteo's heel for tests? It only seemed like a few drops.

As Joseph walked quickly to the station, relieved that he'd missed the rush, a guilty thought crossed his mind. How could he avoid a conversation with Mrs. Charles?

She seemed to have eyes that saw through the walls into his flat, but of course she only had to listen to know when he was practising or pacing the floor. He couldn't explain to her that when he was playing a piece from start to finish—and planning to repeat it immediately before his fingers came to rest on the keyboard—he couldn't bear to be interrupted. She knew he was there so after the first knock, she would wait a minute, then knock again. When he opened the door, she'd have a small piece of information to impart and even kept something back, so there'd be a reason to pop round the following day. It was usually some news about a new line in ready meals in the local supermarket.

She didn't need an excuse for her next visit. A letter addressed to him had been put through her letter box. On the front of the envelope were the two linked hearts of the Blood Transfusion Service. Inside were his details: Joseph Maggiore. Blood Group O. RH positive.

It never occurred to him that he wouldn't be able to give blood for Matteo. It seemed the natural thing to do. But the next time he was by the incubator and they were talking about a transfusion, Joseph put his hand in his pocket, pulled out the donor card and offered it to a junior doctor.

"I'm not at all sure they allow it. They are careful about selecting donors for premature babies. They have to check for antibodies."

"Wait, what are you saying? Wouldn't the best blood be from his father?"

The doctor was looking at the card. Then he looked at the notes on Matteo's incubator.

"Just a moment, Mr. Maggiore."

He went out of the room and Joseph was left waiting. Another doctor came into the room and pulled up two chairs.

"Ah. Come and sit down a minute."

"What's the matter? Is something wrong with Matteo?"

"No, there's nothing new. It's about the blood."

"What about it? I want to give the blood for his next transfusion."

"My colleague—he hasn't a lot of experience here, he might have misled you. I'm afraid it won't be possible."

"Why not?"

"It's never done. We have no facilities to take blood from members of the family and as we explained to you, the selection process is very strict."

"But, as I explain to you, I think his father is the best person to give him the blood."

The doctor is silent. He takes off his glasses, swings them between his thumb and first finger.

"I'm not sure I should be discussing this with you."

"What's there to discuss?"

"I didn't want to go into this, but if it's the only way to persuade you, I'll explain. The problem is that Matteo's blood group is A. You know about the blood groups?"

"Yes. I know something. I know if you give blood it has to match—otherwise the person can die."

"Well, it's a bit more complicated than that. You're right. Mixing blood from two individuals can lead to blood clumping or agglutination. The clumped red cells can crack and cause toxic reactions. This can have fatal consequences."

"So what does this have to do with Matteo?"

"Well, your donor card shows that you are group O. We know that his mother was group B. That was on our records before the baby was born."

"So you're saying you'd rather have someone who is group B, like his mother?"

"No, Mr. Maggiore." He puts his glasses back on. "What I'm saying is this. Matteo's blood group is not compatible with yours. I'm sorry."

The doctor got up and began to walk away.

"Wait a minute. What is 'not compatible'?"

"Let's leave it at that."

"No, I won't leave it. What are you telling me?" He pulled at the doctor's sleeve.

"I thought I'd made it clear."

"You're saying my blood is not the same as Matteo's. Are you telling me he's not my son?"

"Mr. Maggiore, I'm afraid there are certain combinations that are simply not possible. A child whose mother is group B and whose own blood is group A cannot have a father who is group O."

Joseph felt dizzy. He put his head between his legs, grasping at the plastic rim of the seat to stop himself falling off the chair. The room was moving round and someone brought him a glass of water. The doctor had left the room. Joseph was thankful to be alone and as soon as he felt steady he stood up and made his way to the door. He didn't wait for the lift but walked down the stairs, along the corridor and out of the hospital. The cold air hit his face and lashed the tears across his cheeks.

He couldn't believe for a moment that Carla would be unfaithful. She'd cooked for him, ironed his shirts, rolled over to his side of the bed and in the mornings she would pick up his pyjamas from the floor. But what about the evenings when he was playing in concerts and the times he was away? She'd have been alone in the flat. She'd have known when he would be home, that he couldn't be back earlier. It would have been so easy.

Joseph began to torment himself with images of men making love with Carla in their bed. What was he like, this man who was not Group O? Maybe he was tall, fair-haired? Matteo's hair wasn't dark like his parents. But which parents? For Joseph the word had never been plural. He'd been the only one around; the one who went to the hospital every day; who lay awake at night, imagining the worst—that next day Matteo's little body would be lifeless in the incubator.

It's strange how the mind can imitate the switches on a CD player; rewinding to play back happy events, but also fast-

194

forwarding in a tumble of imagined horrors. Joseph was unable to turn off the scenes in front of his eyes: back to Carla drinking coffee with him, putting her arms round him, asking how his concert has gone. And then the whirr of his black imagination: Carla lying underneath another man; Carla making sure the sheets are clean before his return; Carla planning and plotting behind his back. In this grim scenario there was no sign of Sophie. He had convinced himself that his love for Sophie was quite outside his other life, that he could keep the two separate. To justify his infidelity, he had persuaded himself that no-one was harmed by a few secluded meetings in foreign hotels. But what Carla had done was different. She had left him with a question mark that would nag at him for the rest of his life. Every time he looked at Matteo he would be reminded that there was no connection between them, that he was merely a caretaker—in the true sense of the word—not a parent.

For a week Joseph kept away from the hospital. He tried to put Matteo out of his mind but at night he still woke up sweating, reaching for the telephone—and then putting it down again. In the early hours the unit was never in darkness and the nursing staff were always on call. For several days there was no-one phoning to ask if Matteo stopped breathing, and if so, for how many seconds.

Even though he kept his distance, Joseph couldn't blot out the brown eyes and the little wisps of hair that had started growing again. And then he thought of the colour—a soft, light brown. Who did he look like?

CHAPTER 35

Tom drew out thirty pounds and paid the taxi from the airport. He pulled the overnight bag on to his shoulder and ran up the steps, two at a time. As he went into the flat his energy seemed to disappear and he slumped into the leather chair, breathing out like a deflating balloon. The sofa looked back at him accusingly; there were no long legs curled on its cushions; no bags or magazines, tissues or slips of paper that Sophie used to leave around. He was the one who would automatically tidy up, scooping up a glass and putting it in its right place in the cupboard or snatching a scarf and taking it into the bedroom. The living area had to be clear, with nothing around. Sophie had never called him obsessive, but his tidiness had been the subject of many conversations.

"I don't know why you can't just pick up your things and put them away?" he'd ask.

"And why can't you relax when there's anything around? I don't feel the need to remove every object so the place looks like a modern art gallery."

"That's not the point, Sophie. It's minimalist. That's what I'm aiming at."

"But if you clear everything out of your life, you're left with nothing. Like when you cleared your parents' house, after your father died."

"Yes, but my mother was going to live in Spain."

"But after she'd taken the things she needed, you just got rid of the rest. Didn't you want to keep anything? Anything from your childhood?"

"No."

"Don't sulk, darling. I'm not getting at you. I just can't understand this urge to wipe away the past."

"That's not the point. I just don't want Vettriano prints on the walls and little knick-knacks on nests of tables."

Sophie had given in. She'd agreed to his furnishing scheme and tried to learn never to put anything down, when you could put it away. Tom didn't consider that he'd won—just that Sophie had come round to the right way of doing things.

He opened the gliding drawer of the cabinet and took out the newspaper. The date at the top caught his eye: April 4th, exactly three months since Sophie's death. He tried to distract himself by doing the crossword. The interplay of words and their meanings was becoming an obsession. At his side was a thesaurus and even when he wasn't trying to solve an anagram or find a synonym, he loved to choose a word at random and work through parallel meanings. Yet the words he chose were often linked to the state of mind he was trying to avoid: 'End: cease, destroy, decease;' 'Upturn: invert, capsize, overturn, upset, tumble, reverse.' It was the last of these words that made Tom sit up. He was thirty two and behaving as if his life had come to an end. He poured himself a whisky and walked into the bedroom. None of Sophie's possessions had been touched. He decided this was the moment to begin.

He opened the walk-in wardrobe and looked at the rail. While Sophie would happily leave a trail of things in the living room, her clothes were organised in colour sequence just like the stores they'd come from. He remembered how excited she was after her first trip to Bond Street:

"You can't imagine. It's what the French call 'soigné.'"

"So, there are shops, what's special about that?"

"They're like palaces, like temples. They've got these huge glass doors that lead into a world of light and marble."

"And they're so heavy they need to be opened by one of those young men dressed in black from head to toe."

"You're missing the point. Those men are chosen just because they're beautiful. They're not shop assistants; they're probably actors. And what else should they wear but black? You don't understand."

So many of their conversations ended with the words 'you don't understand'. But in spite of the lack of verbal communication when they might have questioned or explained each other's concerns, they hardly ever had a row. Seven years of marriage had brought the relaxed ease that normally came with a silver wedding anniversary. Tom didn't discuss sex with anyone; not his friends, certainly not his parents and even less with his wife. If he were honest, he'd have to admit that it was a slight problem. He put Sophie's reluctance down to a fear of pregnancy. The turning away in bed had only been for a couple of months. Tom was thinking long-term. It was a delicate situation and the most sensible course was to be patient. She might change her mind about having a baby, or stop worrying about the precautions they were taking. Either way it wouldn't take long to rekindle the spark they once had. It never dawned on him that nurturing her wardrobe may have been a substitute for the love she would have lavished on a child.

Tom ran his hand over the clothes. The silk camisoles and La Perla underwear had livened things up for a week or two. But then they'd had the argument about the Nicole Farhi pants which he called mud-coloured and Sophie called taupe. There were fifteen pairs of tailored black trousers. Further along were bias-cut dresses and Armani suits. On the shelves were cashmere sweaters and embroidered satin wraps. The handbags were stacked vertically: the Gucci with the linked Gs, a couple of Louis Vuitton and four by Lulu Guinness. Tom lifted out the hangers and piled everything on to the bed.

He went to find the Yellow Pages and began to leaf through the section on clothes. Vintage? No, that wasn't right, they were modern, almost new. He tried 'Designer Clothes — Second Hand'. The song 'Second Hand Rose' began to boom into his brain. Did Sophie feel that she was second best to her sisters? She'd often complained about wearing cast-offs as a child, but had more than made up for it once she had married Tom. It made him happy that he was doing well enough to give her the money to buy whatever she needed. No, it couldn't be described as 'need'—'requirement, scarcity, desire'—yes, desire, that was nearer to it. Whatever she wanted. It didn't occur to him to offer the clothes to Gemma or Debs. The tops and jackets were all a size 12 — far too small for them. He had a vision of the ugly sisters struggling with a zip or busting a button to close a jacket. But that was hardly fair; the ugliness was only in Sophie's mind. Her sisters were kind and thoughtful. It was just that she had seen them as a threat and had never grown out of her middle child insecurity. But there was another reason for him to dispose of the clothes rather than offering them to her family: he didn't want them to see that most of the items were hardly worn.

After all their conversations, Tom still couldn't understand why Sophie wanted to buy so many outfits and was then content to have them lined up in covered bags which were rarely opened. He was unconvinced by her argument that she was a collector; that the pleasure was in the search and not the public display. At first she genuinely seemed to enjoy looking up-to-date and elegant, but for a few months last year the acquisition seemed almost frenetic. Tom wanted to avoid confrontation, so, as with his other problem, he thought it wiser not to bring up the subject again.

He made an arrangement for someone to come and value the clothes the following day. He was dreading the appointment. He himself had little idea of how much each item was worth and had no total figure in mind. It would have been simpler to take them to a charity shop, but he couldn't bring himself to dispose of them like that—given the amount of effort Sophie had put into acquiring them. The bed was now piled high with clothing. He didn't have the energy to lift it all off so he'd have to sleep on the sofa. He picked up his pyjamas and pulled two other garments out from underneath the pillow.

He was about to close the wardrobe when he saw, tucked in at the back, a bag from Ferragamo in Bond Street. It reminded him for a moment of the time when they were in Lisbon and he'd found the Armani bag from Bond Street in their hotel bedroom. This one had the logo "Ferragamo—Paris, London, Rome" and inside it were three small bags, all with the characteristic rope handles. Each one contained an accessory: a leather key fob with a calfskin strap, a pair of Navigator sunglasses and a belt. Tom' eyes widened as he looked at the bill: Purple python belt: £422. Why had Sophie never taken them out and why were they packed separately? Behind the bags, right in the corner of the wardrobe was a box. Tom took it out and opened it. Inside was a pile of museum catalogues—from every city they'd ever visited. He recognised the Rubens House in Antwerp, the Pinacoteca in Bologna and the Accademia in Florence. On the top was an envelope with a brand new catalogue. It was for a Vermeer exhibition to be held in Bonn and the date was March 15th—two months after Sophie's death. She knew that Tom was planning a business trip then but why would she have bought the catalogue so long in advance? He let it slip from his hands on to the floor.

Tom undressed and looked at his pyjamas. Then he fingered the polo neck top and the loose black trousers that he'd pulled from under the pillow. How many times had he joked about her 'pear shaped bottom'? Every day since January 4th he'd fallen asleep with his arms around her clothes. At first he'd breathed in her scent, deep in the fabric. But now the smell of her presence was fading and even though he buried his face in the soft material she wasn't there. Hardly knowing what he was doing he slid one leg into the black trousers. He pulled them up, stretching them with his other leg and feeling the tightness of the waistband. Then he pulled the polo top over his head and fell asleep in the blackness.

CHAPTER 36

Outside the baby unit was an entryphone for visitors. Joseph always arrived with a feeling of trepidation. The familiar walk through the hospital building to the baby's bedside followed the same pattern every time. The mixture of routine and shock reminded him of the description of an airline pilot's work: 'hours of boredom punctuated by moments of panic.' In the early weeks the surprise was usually bad news—a loss in weight or a threatened infection. Standing by the incubator, he'd peer at the tubes and the beeping monitors that registered every breath; every leap in heart rate. One day he'd arrived to find a tube inserted in Matteo's scalp. The shaving had left a small bald patch, with fine hairs scattered on the sheet. Joseph had tried to pick them up but his eyes were blurred from the tears he'd held back for so long.

He nodded to the sister in charge and went straight over to see the baby. Matteo had progressed from the incubator with five monitors to a new open cot which had only two. A chart showed the date: April 1st, and the infant's weight: 1.8kg/4lbs. To anyone else this was a small baby—at three months, still about half the size of a normal newborn. But for Joseph, the fact that he was living and growing was miracle enough. He lifted him out, took off the woolly hat and undid the doll-size clothes. He held Matteo's toes in his hand and felt the plump warmth of his legs, comparing them to the thin, translucent limbs he'd had when he was born. The baby stared back at him with intense eyes and looked up at a mobile swinging over the cot. Then, as Joseph murmured something to him, a smile of recognition came over Matteo's face. The doctor must have been standing at the door for a few moments watching the two of them, completely absorbed in each other, unaware of anything else around them.

"I think he's ready now."

"Pardon?"

"You can take this little guy home. How are you fixed for the day after tomorrow?"

Joseph pretended he'd misunderstood.

"I'm busy this week."

The doctor ignored the comment and continued:

"Wednesday morning will be fine. We just have to do some final checks and the nurses will fill you in on everything you need to know."

"But I don't know anything. I don't know how to look after him. I can feed him but ..."

"Don't worry. There's a room here so you can spend the next day or so with him. You'll do everything. The nurses will be there in the background in case you need any help."

The reality dawned on Joseph. He had become so used to the hospital environment that he was not prepared to bring Matteo home. He began to mumble:

"But I can't. I'm not ready. I haven't bought anything. I don't have things like a cot or clothes."

The doctor had heard it all before.

"Joseph. Let me tell you something. If I said you could take him home next week, you still wouldn't be ready. It's up here," he said, tapping the side of his head.

He understood that parents of premature babies had no nursery with matching curtains and wallpaper. They were too scared to buy the essential supplies. They certainly had no clothes wrapped in tissue paper. What they had was a fear that they couldn't manage without the support of the nursing staff and the medical equipment. The only way to deal with that fear was to give them no time to think about bringing the baby home.

"So we'll see you tomorrow. Come back with your things and we'll show you where to sleep."

Joseph thought back to the time he was ten years old, hovering on the side of a swimming pool, waiting for the courage to dive in. The teacher's voice was echoing round the walls:

"Vai, vai, vai. Ponti, Massetti, Maggiore—go, go, go."

And he was left crouching there, unable to fling himself in. The teacher's face merged with that of the doctor, as he felt the little push that propelled him towards the water.

*

The cot proved easy to find. The store's baby department provided a list of essentials which ran into two pages. Joseph made a random selection and bought blankets, disposable nappies and wipes. He looked on a rail and found two all-in-one outfits which seemed suitable for a 4 lb baby. Then he picked up a grobag, which sounded more like something for plants. At the other end of the department were the toys. A small child was playing on the floor, pressing buttons that made animal sounds.

Joseph stood staring at sets of building blocks. An assistant appeared at his side.

"Can I help you sir?"

"Yes, I mean, no thank you. I was just looking for ... maybe a train set?"

"Is it for yourself or do you have a child in mind?"

Joseph was embarrassed.

"It's for a baby. Maybe lego is better. More easy to put together than a train track?"

"Well, these lego sets are a bit complicated. Does the baby have specially good co-ordination?"

Joseph moved to a display of soft toys: lions, monkeys and a tiger with a long cuddly tail.

"Do you have anything a bit less ... tropical, like a teddy bear?"

"Yes, they're over here. You need one that's washable."

The bears came in all sizes, with fur or a woolly coat. The biggest one was three feet long and white with a blue ribbon. Joseph picked it up and hugged it.

"This'll do. It's soft. I think he'll like it."

By this time there was a queue at the counter. Joseph went back to collect the buggy he'd chosen and waited to pay. He looked at the label and wondered at the words on the card: 'Travel System', not sure of what system he'd need to get all the parcels piled on the top. He was wheeling it along, with bags hanging from the handles and falling from the seat as he remembered the cot. He went back to the till and arranged for it all to be sent to the collection point on the ground floor.

When he got home, the first thing to do was to assemble the cot. Joseph assumed that the words 'flat pack' probably referred to the size, meaning it was suitable for a small flat. He struggled with the screws and nuts for half an hour. Fingers that could ripple up and down a keyboard were no use with a screwdriver. The diagrams were easy enough for a child to understand, but that didn't mean that you could hold the side pieces firm and fix the base without the whole thing collapsing on the floor. Stepping over the metal sliders and assorted screws, he abandoned the task and addressed himself to the problem of clothes. There was apparently a place in Skelmersdale that specialised in premature baby wear. He couldn't even pronounce the name of the town, let alone decide what was needed. He ordered five sleep suits and made them promise to send them by first class post.

Joseph looked around the flat and set about clearing up the mess. He'd cleaned the area round his bed and the kitchen when he realised there was no baby milk. He threw down the cloth and rushed out to the local chemist, where he was presented with a bewildering choice: different brands of formula—powdered or made up. It was midnight when the cot was assembled and Joseph finally fell into a deep sleep, dreaming of what was needed: fingernail clippers, bulb nose aspirator, digital thermometer, pacifier—he hadn't got any of them. He woke up and bumped his leg on the cot, forgetting it was inches away from his bed.

He went over to the piano and tried to settle his nerves by playing a Chopin Nocturne. He began the C minor from memory but found the plaintive melody did little to improve his mood. Searching for the music for the one in D flat, he came across some notes he'd made, reminding him why he needed to keep working on it.

He'd never thought of singing while he played but someone had said 'If you can't sing the ornaments as fast as you're playing them, then you're too fast.' He dismissed this piece of advice—of course notes couldn't come out of his mouth as fast as the ones his fingers were playing. He decided to forget about speed and think only of the melody. He needed to capture the elusive essence of night-time in the theme but found himself carried away by the soft passages and the moment of pure magic when the key turned into the relative minor in bar 10. What he loved was the change in tone: starting with his fingers stroking the keys, slowing, almost drifting as if sleep were about to come, and then a dramatic return to a repeat of the melody and the thunderous dominance of the right hand.

He rarely linked a piano piece to his state of mind, but from this moment the hypnotic lyricism of the Chopin Nocturne would always remind him of the nights before he brought Matteo home.

CHAPTER 37

For the next two days Joseph hardly left the hospital. He was installed in a small room across the corridor and Matteo's cot was wheeled into the corner. Not knowing what to pack, he'd chosen the wrong selection. The new blankets stayed in their wrapping as bedding was provided, but the two sleep suits he'd brought were quite inadequate to cope with the constant change of clothes. He learned how to push the baby's hand into a sleeve, pulling it through without tugging at the fabric. Feeding was done eight times a day. The 2oz milk went down very slowly. Halfway through the bottle, a nurse came and showed him how to circle the baby's back with his fingers. A new mother who had been in the company of friends' babies, might have known how to release the wind. What did a father know about such things? The first bath left Joseph with soaked trousers as he crossed the room to find a towel, with Matteo dripping water all over the floor.

Every few hours, when he'd finished all the tasks, he fell exhausted on to the bed, with Matteo face down on his bare chest. Only then did he plug in the Schubert CD, blocking his ears with the sound of a sonata, knowing that he could feel without hearing whether or not the baby was breathing.

On Wednesday morning Joseph slipped out of the hospital and returned with three cakes: a lemon cheesecake, a strawberry tart and cocoa-covered tiramisu. He handed them to his favourite nurses and stood, faintly embarrassed, as one offered to change Matteo into his new clothes, while another kept giving snippets of advice:

"Don't forget to wake him up for his feed. Every three hours. Even if he's sound asleep."

"Put him to sleep on his side. He likes it better."

"Hey Matteo, who's a big boy now?"

"We're going to miss you, aren't we?"

Joseph asked a stream of questions, avoiding the one that concerned him most. The doctor pre-empted his thoughts:

"Have you got everything you need?"

"I haven't got any equipment" snapped Joseph.

"I know what you're thinking. The apnoea monitor. You're worried he'll stop breathing."

"Do you think I should buy one, or can I hire one?"

"You don't need it. We think he's ready to go home so we've had him off it for days now. He's got to lead a normal life and he won't if there's a monitor beeping behind his cot."

"But how do you know he won't suddenly stop breathing again?"

"Joseph, do I know when I'm going to stop breathing? It's not in our hands."

One of the nurses broke the silence and produced a camera. Another passed round one of the cakes.

"Hey, Matteo, be a good boy. Come and see us soon."

Joseph walked slowly to the door, stopping as he went past the intensive care room and turning to acknowledge the waves and smiles. He pulled the blanket round the baby, got into a taxi and closed his eyes.

*

He'd been in the flat for about an hour when the doorbell rang. He went over to the cot and turned Matteo over so he was lying on his other side. Then he went to open the door. It was Mrs. Charles offering help.

"Beautiful. He's beautiful. Carla would have been so proud of him. Who does he look like? He hasn't got your hair colouring."

Joseph couldn't quite explain to himself why he'd turned Matteo over so no-one could see the bald patch. Before he knew what he was saying he blurted out:

"He doesn't have a lot of hair. They shaved it off."

Joseph immediately regretted his brusque response. His neighbour had made an innocent comment about the baby's hair colour. Joseph couldn't forget that half of his head had no hair at all. He wanted visitors to see Matteo as a perfect baby. He might still be small but it was important that there should be no visible defects.

Mrs. Charles had no idea what was going through his mind. She was pulling something out of a bag.

"I've got something for him."

Joseph unwrapped the parcel. Inside was a small brown teddy bear with a tartan ribbon and a gift tag that said: "Much love, Winifred Charles."

"Oh, dear. I see he's got one already" she said, looking at the large bear that Joseph had bought the previous day.

"Well, I think I made a mistake. It'll be years till he can get his arms round that one. Yours is great. I'll put it in the cot with him."

When Mrs. Charles had gone Joseph moved the baby seat into his bedroom and looked at Matteo's tiny face; the eyelashes closed on perfect white skin, the fingers of one hand opening and closing. There was no sound in the room apart from the long, slow breaths of sleep. And then a whisper:

"Eh, tesoro. It's just you and me now."

CHAPTER 38

In the middle of the night Joseph was often awake, nervous that he'd let Matteo sleep longer than three hours. Listening to the heavy breathing in the darkened room, he let his mind wander from concerns about the baby to past worries that were more of his own making. Thoughts that in daytime were logical and positive turned sour in the hours after midnight. He pulled up the covers and minutes later threw them off as his body raged with imagined heat. One night, after a particularly restless session, he crept out of the bedroom and sat at the kitchen table, leafing through a ring binder full of critics' notes on his performances.

Reviews of classical music have something in common with descriptions of fine wine. An expert may liken a Chablis to flint and wet stones, or describe a Claret as having a blackcurrant nose, but to the uninitiated such writing seems pretentious. It's so hard to match a word to a scent or a taste. In the same way music critics try to bring a touch or a sound to life but it's no easy task. The pages in the binder were a mixture of authentic reviews from the national papers and the fictions devised by Sophie to describe his non-existent concerts in Europe. The invented reviews were concocted from the internet and included sentences that had been used to describe other performers. Sophie had discovered that Glenn Gould was not above writing his own words in praise of his latest CD and so she felt no shame in lifting the odd sentence and applying it to Joseph and his technique:

"... a brilliant young virtuoso ... an amazing tour de force, his playing as fleet and joyous as the wind, still preserving needle-sharp clarity."

At one time Sophie had been looking for a review she could copy for a page purporting to come from the Corriere della Sera. She'd found a critique of Brendel's Moonlight Sonata which Joseph rather liked, but Sophie could hardly stop laughing as she read it out:

"Brendel imbues the Moonlight's famous Adagio with more rhetorical wiggle room and shapely base lines. The Allegretto is sharper—more pointed—and lighter in being. The Appassionata recaptures the biting accents, angularity and daring of his previous work, but in other ways it's less pingy than before."

Carla had never suspected that the printed reviews were not genuine; she had no reason to think they were anything but authentic. Yet for a week or so after his return from Florence last July Carla's behaviour had changed. She seemed to be checking his post and listening to his phone conversations and even once mentioned that Richard was concerned about his foreign bookings.

The cuttings triggered other memories of the deceptions they had invented. Sophie needed the museum catalogues to show that she was spending her time at exhibitions. Usually they were sent to Joseph in London and he would pack them in his overnight bag. But once or twice Carla opened his post and he had to throw them away, answering her question with a shrug and a suggestion that they must have been sent to the wrong person.

When Joseph returned from his trips abroad he brought his wife small gifts of surprisingly good taste. Each one had been chosen with ultimate care: silver-plated tea light holders or a calfskin diary. The one she loved best was a herb cutter—a mezzaluna in stainless steel. But Joseph had no time to go to boutiques while he was away. His few days were spent waiting in dismal bedrooms for Sophie to come; and then, when she was there, shopping was the last thing on their mind. So it was Sophie who looked for just the right pair of drop earrings or a bracelet made from fine silver wire. She'd buy it in London, take it to Belgium or Italy, and give it to Joseph to take back. The one piece that Joseph had bought—the opal heart necklace—was never intended for Carla at all. It was this small object, a birthday present meant for Sophie, that caused him more guilt than any of the lies he'd told.

CHAPTER 39

The hours of broken sleep played havoc with Joseph's daytime routine. He'd worked out a practice regimen that took no longer than an hour, so he could run through it while Matteo had a morning nap. Mrs. Charles offered to look after the baby for a few hours each afternoon and he was then free to spend time on note learning and the constant refining of sound. He should have been tackling scale and arpeggio passages, and experimenting with pedalling and chord balancing, but he could hardly keep himself awake. At night he'd fall asleep dreaming of feeding, nappy changing and taking clothes to the launderette.

In the mornings Joseph opened bleary eyes to make up the bottles of powdered milk. He'd done it so often he knew automatically how many scoops to mix with 300 mls of water.

But one day he added an extra scoop to each bottle. He must have known that with more powder the milk would be too rich and it might have a drastic effect, so why did he do it? At the moment of mixing he wasn't just feeling tired. He was full of resentment. He was angry at Matteo, at the world and especially Carla. He put four of the bottles in the fridge and picking up the fifth, went to lift the baby out of the cot. Matteo leaned forward eagerly, his hands tapping the plastic, sucking hard to get that first rush of the day.

As the milk squeezed through the teat, Joseph came to his senses, unable to believe what he had done. He pulled at the bottle and threw it on the floor. Matteo burst into tears; a loud wail followed by a silence as he held his breath for what seemed like minutes. Then he let out another yell, choking and gasping. Joseph rushed to the kitchen to make up a new batch of milk. While the water boiled he remembered how the nurses had taken such care inserting the feed tube through Matteo's tiny nostril, making sure it went straight down to his stomach. They never made mistakes.

He picked up Matteo and walked round the flat, looking for the teddy. He finally found it propped up by the bath. When he'd folded the baby's arms round the bear, he whispered in his ear to calm the sobbing:

"It's OK, it's OK. I'm sorry."

Matteo pulled at the tartan ribbon and began sucking. It was a long ribbon and he passed it through his mouth, soaking each part of it, until he came to the end. Then he did it again from the other end, slurping happily as the sodden ribbon passed his lips. Matteo had become inseparable from the bear, but it wasn't so much the furry face that he loved, but the ritual of sucking and sliding the ribbon.

"You like him, no? What shall we call him? I know, let's call him Fred—after Winifred. But we'd better not tell her."

At that moment Winifred Charles knocked at the door.

"Is everything all right?"

"Yes, we're fine."

He opened the door, but not wide enough to make it an invitation to come in. Mrs. Charles stood there:

"I heard the baby crying. That's not like him."

"No, I don't let him cry. Only, this time. I didn't have his feed ready."

"How's the piano going? You never play in the evenings any more."

"Well, I'm really too tired."

"What you need is some more help."

"No, I'm fine. I can manage."

"Tell you what. Why don't you let my granddaughter come and babysit for you? Annabel's almost sixteen and she's good with babies. She could look after Matteo while you do the concerts."

Joseph thanked her and agreed to check his diary and speak to Annabel. The offer of help coincided with a series of phone messages from Richard. The relationship between them was a typical masculine one: conversations relating only to bookings, with no reference to what had gone before. Initially there had been a coolness after Richard had learned about the non-existent concerts abroad, but there was no discussion and after a while they'd continued as before, with his agent finding the work and Joseph paying the commission.

Richard seemed to have no idea of the pressures: no conception of what it was like, trying to bring up a baby single-handed and maintain a place on the concert circuit. As Joseph failed to return his calls he turned up one day in the middle of the afternoon.

"Don't you want to hear about these plans I've got?"

Richard was wearing a smart suit. Joseph could tell it was new because the pleat at the back of the jacket was held together with a cross of cotton thread.

"Come on then. Tell me."

"First you have to get yourself a website. Then we have to be more inventive in chasing the work."

"I don't have the energy for all this, Richard."

"That's the point. You just have to get back to playing the piano. I'm the one who's doing the organising. It wasn't a good idea when you were doing it on your own."

Joseph preferred to ignore the reference to his imaginary concerts. Richard was straightening his tie:

"First of all, I'm going to change my name. Richard Adams isn't much of a name if I'm representing a world-renowned pianist. From now on I'm going to be called Riccardo Speranza."

"Where did you get that name from? Speranza means hope."

"Exactly, I'm being positive. Now stop interrupting."

"Wait a minute," said Joseph. "I change my name from Giuseppe because it's easier to pronounce an English name, and you're wanting to do the reverse."

Richard ignored his comment and went into the kitchen to get a drink of water.

Joseph called after him:

"The glasses are all dirty."

To his surprise Richard was already coming back with the water in one of the crystal glasses he and Carla had got for a wedding present. As if to explain why he was so at home in the kitchen, Richard blurted out:

"Carla was too small to reach the top of the cupboard. She asked me to do it once, when I was here waiting for you."

For a moment neither of them spoke, with the heavy memory of Carla in both their minds. Richard broke the silence:

"Here's what we're going to do. Most concert halls will have bookings far into the future and won't be able to offer you anything. But I've got an idea: you could do some workshops for young people, playing in top venues for an hour before the main concert. The piece you focus on will be on the concert programme so it'll attract a big audience, as well as the twenty or so students who will pay to be taught. It's not so ridiculous. It could work. At £20 each, that's £400 for an evening."

While they were talking Matteo was getting noisy, sometimes gurgling, then beginning to cry. Joseph went to pick him up and Richard watched as he carried the baby on his hip and went to heat up a bottle. It took fifteen minutes till the last drops had gurgled through the teat. Matteo pulled the bottle from his mouth and grinned at his father.

"Can I hold him?" asked Richard tentatively.

"Sure. He likes it if you talk to him. Preferably in Italian, Mr. Speranza."

Richard laughed and put out his hands. Matteo was wriggling as the unfamiliar man held him at arm's length, making sure there was no contact between milky fingers and the new suit. As Richard handed him back, Matteo gave a lurch and threw up the whole of his feed. A creamy liquid stain poured over Joseph's sleeve and dripped on to the carpet.

"O Dio, not again. He can't keep the milk down."

No-one knew about that disastrous day when Joseph had mixed up the wrong feed. Since then he'd been scrupulously careful to get the measurements exactly right. He'd never given him the concentrated milk, yet for some reason Matteo was vomiting five or six times a day.

Richard made an excuse and let himself out. Joseph looked for clean pyjamas and put the baby in his cot. Five minutes later Matteo was crying; not the loud yells of hunger, but a kind of sobbing interspersed with silence. When Joseph went in he found that Matteo had been sick again, all over the sheets. Not knowing whether to deal first with the carpet or the bedclothes, Joseph let out a yell:

"Carla, for heaven's sake. I need you!"

CHAPTER 40

In furniture showrooms they wrap a couple of books in white paper and arrange them on a shelf. Woven lengths of fabric are draped over beds as throws. There are lilies in a vase on a glass table, but no sign of real life; no crumpled magazines, no stained teacups or apple cores wrapped in bits of tissue. Tom had been aiming at such perfection ever since he'd lived at home with his parents. Their house in Surbiton was no different from the others in the street and perhaps that was why their son was so critical. The living room was full of what his mother called 'treasures'. On every surface was an array of china ornaments, glass animals, vases and miniatures. She collected replicas of everything from shoes to cottages—as long as the item was small, it could claim a place on a window sill or shelf. And of course all these items needed dusting. Every day his mother would flick round with a multi-coloured 'magic duster' which looked to him more like candy floss that had gone wrong. Once a week each object would be removed, washed and replaced in exactly the same place. When his parents came to the flat in Greville Place they wondered if perhaps he could do with pictures—not the kind he bought for his hotels—but maybe a Degas print or one of Vincent van Gogh's Starry Night paintings. He tried to explain to them that the sand-coloured walls needed no decoration.

A gust of air blew through the open window, ballooning the floating curtains. Tom rearranged them and reflected on how good they had looked in the ochre sun in Bologna. Now they looked pasty in the cold light of Maida Vale. With the wardrobe empty and the bathroom bare of toiletries Tom began to feel uneasy. It was as if Sophie had never been there. He was finding it hard to remember what it was like when she padded through the rooms in her silk dressing gown. The Barcelona chair stood solidly black and buttoned, hardly ever used. He ate at a single bar stool in the kitchen and took cups of tea into the bedroom where he automatically turned on the television and fell asleep to the sound of the weatherman warning of showers in the North East.

Tom could go days without speaking. The telephone answering machine rarely had a flashing light. There were no messages. No-one to ring back. His appointments were all confirmed by email so there were days when he didn't open his mouth; that is, until he discovered the comfort of one-sided conversations.

As he walked in the door he'd shout:

"Sophie baby I'm home. I know you're not, but I'll tell you about my day anyway."

At meals he balanced the newspaper against the side of his bowl of pasta and discussed the headlines. When he opened his post he read the letters and responded out loud. Anyone listening would have thought he was speaking into a dictating machine. In bed he put his arms round the pillow and whispered things he didn't want anyone else to hear.

Weekends were the worst, with no incentive to leave the silence of the flat. Tom awoke to a grey Saturday in June. He gazed out of the window, staring at the steel sky. With nothing planned for the day and no appointments for the week ahead, he began to dress and by mistake took out two pairs of underpants. Instead of putting one back in the drawer he changed his mind and pulled down a small leather bag. He threw in the pants and stopped for a moment to finish dressing. Then he added shirts, pyjamas and socks and zipped up the bag. A quick calculation told him it would be best to take three of everything.

Without waiting for a change of heart, he phoned for a taxi and opened his computer to scroll down a list of cities served by British Airways. He decided against Abu Dhabi, Addis Ababa and Berlin and moved on to Brussels. He'd missed the 7.25 and the 7.30. Could that be right? Two in five minutes? There was probably a rush hour for European commissioners at that time in the morning. How about Casablanca? No, he wouldn't find much work there. There seemed to be flights almost on the hour to Geneva. He continued to click the keys till he came to flight times for Madrid and Milan. The doorbell rang and Tom closed his computer and pushed the newspaper into the back of the bag. The pavement was shiny from the rain and he almost slipped as he stepped into the taxi.

"Heathrow, please."

"Which terminal sir?"

"Well, let's think. How about Terminal One?"

"Where are you flying to, sir?"

"That's a good question."

Tom settled back in his seat. The driver, just starting his shift, was eager to talk:

"Going for a bit of a holiday, then?"

"No."

"I fancy Ibiza. Ever been there?"

"No, I hate the sun. I'd rather go to Alaska."

Tom's reply had the desired effect. The driver looked in the mirror and saw that his passenger had closed his eyes. No chance of a discussion of yesterday's Arsenal/West Ham match. There was silence as they drove along the Westway with Tom dozing until they entered the tunnel at Heathrow. He paid the taxi, went up to the Mezzanine level and found an internet connection. A computer search for hotels in three cities came up with several that looked due for refurbishment. Perhaps the owners would be in need of new artwork? He scribbled down the addresses, made a careful note of the spellings for possible contacts and put away his laptop. An early lunch was the next item on his agenda. The cafe was far from full and he had a choice of several empty tables. It took him only minutes to read through the menu and when the waitress came over, he ordered straight away:

"Onion soup and steak frites, please."

Leaving his newspaper on the table, he said:

"I'll be back in a minute. Oh, and can you bring me a glass of Merlot as well?"

Ten minutes later he returned to his place, just as the waitress was putting down a bowl of croutons for the soup. He looked at the ticket he'd just bought: MAD 14.30. The airport code made him smile. With a bit of luck he'd make it to the boarding gate by one forty five and arrive in Madrid in the late afternoon. He planned to check into a hotel near the Prado. Sophie would have loved that. There seemed to be a chain that was sprouting a new hotel in Madrid every month. Tom could set up meetings for Monday, be back in London the next day and spend the rest of the week working out which artists to approach.

He paid the bill and put down a generous tip, leaving the newspaper on the table. He'd read the colour magazine and the travel section but reckoned the Arts pages would help to pass the time on the plane. Once he was settled in his seat, feeling the warm glow of the wine and the pleasure of a plate of food that hadn't been burnt or undercooked, he began to leaf through the paper. There was a photograph of a man who seemed vaguely familiar. Under the picture was a reference to a forthcoming concert at the Wigmore Hall in August. The name of the pianist was Joseph Maggiore. And then it came back to him: this was the man he'd met in the cafeteria the day Sophie had her accident. Tom had no idea that Maggiore was so successful. He'd mentioned something about playing the piano but apart from that seemed rather silent. Perhaps it would be a good idea to book a ticket and hear him play?

CHAPTER 41

Joseph was in the green room preparing for the Wigmore Hall concert. He was to open with a Nocturne by John Field and continue with three pieces by Albeniz. None of these presented a problem; he'd spent many hours working on the melodic side of the Nocturne, trying to get to the essence of what had been called a 'song without words'. The Spanish pieces were outside his normal repertoire. The composer had talked of 'colour, sunlight and the flavour of olives'. All he knew was that Granados called for a rhythmic left hand and rapid fingering in the right. He'd mastered the dramatic opening of Navarra, keeping in his head the image of a world-famous guitarist, playing the same notes. The third piece, Mallorca, had a slow, pensive mood—themes he'd played over and over in his saddest moments.

It was the Mozart that was making him nervous. He'd played the sonatas in public several times before but was always aware of the expectation in the audience, knowing that many of them would be comparing his performance to the edited pyrotechnic of sound they could hear at home on CD. It was this thought, and not the baby, that had given him a restless night with only four hours sleep.

Just before dawn he'd dreamed that he was walking away from the concert hall, in the wrong direction, wearing a bow tie but no shirt. Frantically searching for the right clothes, he came across a piano at the side of the road, sat down to play and found his fingers were covered with glue. The next scene was in the concert hall where he was fiddling with the piano stool, unable to keep it still.

Joseph shook his head and brought himself back to reality. The audience was waiting. A cigarette would have helped. Although Carla disapproved of his smoking habit he'd always had one dangling on an ashtray on the piano lid. Taking a drag between movements was routine when he was practising. In a concert he never gave it a thought until he came to the end of the final movement. Then he couldn't wait. To solve the problem of fumbling with packets and lighters, he arranged to have someone stand by with a lighted cigarette, as soon as he came off stage. Then he could feel that tender joyous expansion of the chest before going back for an encore.

He took one last look at the score, put on his jacket and walked out into the hall. In the lonely walk up to the piano his eyes automatically took in the half of the audience that could see his fingers on the keyboard. How many of them had an awareness of the music? And what about the ones in the first few rows? They could read the lettering on the side of the Steinway and were close enough to count the brass studs on the leather piano stool. Minutes before they were an amorphous mass; groups of people having a drink in the bar, settling in their seats and shuffling their programmes. Now it was his job to make them feel he was playing specially for them, though for him it was the result of a routine. If he'd got the progression right—'learn, practise, perform'—they would be satisfied. The nerves and panic oozed away once he took his eyes off the audience. He produced a confident opening to the Nocturne and moved without effort into the Spanish pieces.

In the interval he couldn't allow himself to relax. He had the Mozart score in front of him. He would have liked to run his fingers through the opening of the B Flat allegro. Instead he phoned home.

"Hi Annabel. How's Matteo?"

"OK Mr. Maggiore. He's had some food but he won't take his bottle."

"I know, it's a new stuff. The milk was making him sick, so he's been put on soya milk. I forgot to tell you."

"He's got a bit of a cold too, I expect that's making it worse. He's so snuffly, he can't suck properly."

"Annabel, I've got to go. I'll call you later."

Joseph put down the phone and walked back into the hall. He closed his eyes for a moment and cleared his mind of all thoughts of home. He rolled into the first bars. One of Sophie's reviews might have called the phrasing 'smooth' and the touch 'a buttery lightness'. With barely a pause he moved into the flowing melody of the andante and by the time his fingers rested on the keys at the end of the last movement he began to wonder why he'd been nervous and how he could ever have thought he'd forget the notes. When he stood up he could sense the audience appreciation of the demanding score. The applause was reassuring. He knew by their reaction that he'd touched on what lay underneath the glittering surface of Mozart's notes. How glad he was not to have chosen the Chopin. He simply hadn't practised enough to achieve the right amount of emotion and technical skill needed to pull it off. As the lights came up and he stood looking out into the hall, he felt the confidence slipping away again, wondering how he had managed to conquer the feelings of a panicked father and project an image of a competent pianist.

After two encores he rushed out to look for a cab. He was standing on the pavement when he was stopped by a young man. His first impression was of someone tall, with fair hair and a face with prominent bones. Joseph caught a glimpse of elegant shirt cuffs. The man was talking at great speed:

"I don't suppose you remember. My name's Tom. We met at St. Mary's. In the cafeteria. You were telling me about your career."

"Ye ... es" said Joseph, trying to remember the man and the conversation.

"You know, both our wives were in the intensive care unit. My wife was brought in after an accident. She died. Poor Sophie, she didn't stand a chance. The car was coming so fast and the road was slippery."

The blood drained from Joseph's face. He opened his mouth but no words came out. Did he say his name was Tom? It couldn't be. The man was waiting for him to say something.

"Your wife, Sophie, she died. When?"

"The day we met. They told me just after you left the intensive care unit."

By the time Joseph had composed himself it was too late. The thoughts in his mind had been transferred to the expression on his face. It was like a blank television screen bursting into colour. His confused words made the picture even clearer.

"But what happened? When did she ... ? How? Was she ill?"

"No, I told you, she was hit by a car."

How many messages had he left? Five, ten? Now he understood why she hadn't responded. Joseph was trying to remember the last time he'd spoken to her. It was a few months after the disastrous trip to Lisbon. The man was talking again, saying something about the police and how they wouldn't prosecute the driver. How could he be so calm? Joseph's hand was shaking. He reached for a cigarette and tried to keep the lighter steady as he took in a deep breath. He looked at Tom, the Tom he'd never known, the one who criticised Sophie, who made her feel inadequate. But this man had a pleasant looking face, good looking almost, with his pointed chin and long, straight nose. Joseph felt a rush of questions forming in his mind. When he was making love to Sophie, did she ... did she compare him to Tom, feeling the difference in their height, the growth of their beards? Did she prefer the hair that was fair? What was she thinking when she stroked his own dark eyebrows? He'd never asked her; never thought that she too, could be tormented over the comparison between two lovers. He was trying to remember what Sophie had told him of Tom but all he could think of was the way their affair had ended.

CHAPTER 42

There had been no goodbye, no exchange of promises. Joseph tried to go over events in order. When he was making frantic attempts to prepare a festive meal for Christmas, he still had Sophie constantly in his mind. He remembered sending her a text saying "Buon Natale. I love you."

She wasn't picking up her phone. Later he checked to see if she had replied, making the excuse of going out for a cigarette. He left another message. Her silence was bewildering. As he walked back home he had no idea that she had played and replayed his words and that she was listening with tears pouring down her face.

The next day Carla was ill. In the week that followed Joseph was concerned and by the time he took her into hospital, he was so worried that all other thoughts had gone from his mind. Waiting by her bedside, while she hovered in and out of consciousness, Joseph took out his mobile, moved his fingers over the numbers and then put it away again. How could he expect Sophie to welcome the occasional phone call? How could he go on treating Carla as second best?

And then, there was the birth and the death. After the rollercoaster came crashing to the ground all thoughts of Sophie were pushed out of his mind. Months later there were moments when Joseph was alone with Matteo, or when he was rocking him to sleep at night, when he thought of picking up the phone again. In his dreams there was another pair of arms to hold the baby; the comfort of sharing his worries. But he knew it was hopeless. Sophie had been adamant on the subject of babies—and especially Carla's baby.

*

Tom seemed to be waiting for a response. Joseph closed his eyes. Memories of Sophie were flashing into his head: a few blonde hairs on the floor of a shower, the way she laughed when he mangled an English phrase, the white cotton robe that had no fastening. There was no picture of a Sophie who was dead, lying blue on a hospital bed.

He missed the beginning of the sentence but opened his eyes to see Tom looking at him, speaking almost casually:

"... strange, wasn't it, meeting like that in the hospital and now here we are again."

"O Dio" said Joseph to himself. "Does he know? Has he listened to the messages?"

CHAPTER 43

Annabel was distraught when Joseph finally arrived home, an hour later than promised. Matteo was crying and there were drops of blood on the floor. It was every babysitter's nightmare—the parent coming home to a scene of chaos, with the teenager unable to deal with a simple nosebleed. But it wasn't that simple. At first it was a spattering of blood on Matteo's pyjamas; then wads of cotton wool became saturated and slipped out. After an hour there was no sign that the bleeding would ever stop. Joseph tried laying Matteo on his back, wiping his face with a damp cloth, murmuring to him to stop the crying.

"Eh, tesoro, sono qui, sono qui. I'm here. I'm not going anywhere. It'll stop soon."

Matteo started choking and Joseph could no longer see if the blood was coming from his nose or mouth. He put his arms round him, stuffed some money and keys into a back pocket and rushed out of the flat to call a cab. Then he realised he'd forgotten to bring Fred and went back again to get the teddy out of the cot. They arrived at King's College hospital in minutes. Joseph leapt out of the taxi, holding Matteo and the teddy with one hand and reaching in his pocket for money with the other. At the information desk he was directed to a nurse who examined Matteo briefly and told them to wait. A notice explained that patients in the emergency area were not seen in the order they arrived. The more serious cases were dealt with first.

Joseph sat on the hard plastic seat and settled Matteo on the chair next to him. He was aware of people staring at the baby's blood-stained T-shirt and tear-stained face. A woman next to him offered him a handful of tissues. He looked down, embarrassed at his spattered white evening shirt and twisted bow tie.

They'd been there about half an hour when Joseph realised he was in for a long wait. He'd left in such a hurry he'd brought no milk or toys. Doctors were scurrying between cubicles and an uncomfortable silence settled over the patients listening for their names to be called. The waiting area was filled with the air of unwashed armpits and the humid heat of a late summer evening. Joseph went over to a machine and bought a bar of milk chocolate and broke off a piece. Matteo leaned forward to grasp the rest of the bar and waved it in the air. In between licks he offered the melting stub to various unsmiling faces. Joseph lifted him on to his knee and when the wriggling started, he began to pace around. He kept walking, round and round the waiting area, long after Matteo's eyelids started to flicker, until his breathing had slowed to a sleepy rhythm. Would it be worth risking a change of movement to sit down again? He lowered himself carefully on to a seat, checking to see that the baby was asleep and moving the soggy ribbon that drooped across his arm. The bleeding had stopped.

The sight of Matteo's blood brought back memories of his first transfusion at St. Mary's. Not that he was losing blood then—the staff came to make a tiny prick every few days and took the samples off to the lab. Who knows what he was thinking as the needle pierced the skin? There was no open-mouth cry, no screwing up of the face. Crying was something normal babies did, not ones with small lung capacity. An older child would have put his feelings into words. A child with a serious disease, in hospital for weeks or months, would object to the intrusion and ask their parents to tell the bad people to go away. Matteo only shivered as they took the blood from his heel or his ankle—Joseph couldn't remember which. His thoughts were beginning to go down a road he wanted to avoid.

To take his mind off the whole question of the blood transfusion, Joseph picked up a copy of Hello Magazine. Why were people so interested in the weddings of soap stars, the homes of film actors? He flicked through the pages and stopped at an article about a footballer throwing a two-million pound party. It took a full ten minutes to read about the quantities of caviar and champagne that were consumed, the white silk marquee large enough to house a thousand guests and the parking arrangements for the private helicopters. Chefs had been flown in from Chicago and Paris to prepare a meal that included an oyster soufflé and lobster risotto. Beef of unparalleled quality, from a herd of specially reared black cattle, had been obtained direct from Tokyo. The cost of each mouthful of the wagyu steak worked out at over three pounds. As Joseph put down the magazine, he realised that the ten-minute anaesthetic of a visit into a fantasy world was already wearing off. His thoughts were racing back to the time when he had offered to give his own blood for Matteo's transfusion.

CHAPTER 44

It was midnight in the A & E department. When Matteo's name was finally called he was fast asleep. In the cubicle the baby woke up to a bright light shining in his face. He struggled to free his arms as his father held them down. The junior doctor was trying to find out the cause of such a violent nose bleed. He had been trained to consider several possibilities. A quick examination made it clear there was no injury or fracture. It could be sinusitis or anaemia. He would need to run tests to see if it was leukaemia or a tumour. At least in a child of that age he could eliminate typhoid fever, hepatitis and the over use of cocaine. The bleeding had eventually stopped, but not before Joseph had imagined a host of explanations. Carla would have been even more inventive, as she always thought the worst and created the most serious outcome from the slightest pimple or sneeze.

The reality in children was that most nosebleeds were caused by a little finger picking the nostril. In Matteo's case it was a pea. He'd been crawling under the table and found several interesting objects: a piece of fluff that didn't taste good and a round green thing that was dry and must have been there for days. Not wanting to risk another disappointing flavour, he'd pushed the pea up his nose. The doctor removed it with a long instrument that looked like elongated tweezers.

When they got home it was nearly one o'clock. Joseph shifted the weight of the sleeping baby on his shoulder and felt in his pocket for the key to the front door. He went straight to the bedroom and Matteo stirred as Joseph tried to remove the stained T-shirt. He raised it gently and pulled one arm at a time out of the sleeves. Then he lifted it over the baby's head, stretching the neck open to make sure he didn't catch his ear or squeeze too tightly over his hair. He licked a layer of chocolate off the baby fingers and eased on a clean top. Matteo barely moved as he was lowered into the cot, with Fred tucked under one arm, and his fingers twined round the teddy's ribbon. Joseph covered them both with a sheet and as he leaned over he breathed in the sweet smell of baby hair mixed with the aroma of chocolate and grubby fingers.

As Joseph stood looking down on Matteo he wondered what it was that made a small dependent baby so absorbing. If someone had told him that the focus of his life would change immediately he held his child he would have dismissed it as women's magazine emotion. Yet since that first time in the hospital when Matteo had stretched out his arm, trying to make his tiny hand close around Joseph's finger, he recognised a falling in love that intensified with each week. He tried to separate the joy of holding the little body from the terror that any moment it might be taken away—that he'd go in one day and find that Matteo was dying. He imagined every scenario: an infection that wouldn't respond to antibiotics; heart failure; a malfunction of the bowel or most likely, that the breathing would simply stop.

The nurses had encouraged him to take Matteo out of the incubator and lay him naked on his own bare chest, in what they called 'kangaroo care'. In those moments it wasn't thoughts of football or male bonding that passed through Joseph's mind. He would stroke the spot where Matteo's hair curled at the nape of his neck and run his fingers along the bone thin legs, wondering if they would ever have the strength to stand or walk. Yet in seven months the baby was growing and moving in a progression of competence. He had learned how to select and grasp, wrapping his fingers round an object, bringing it to his mouth to get the feel of it. He'd discovered how to hold things in two hands, to shake and rattle. He'd begun to move, crawling with increasing speed and confidence, turning his head as if to say 'look at me, I've found out how the legs and arms work'. He could search the floor for something he had dropped; tug at Fred's furry legs and drag him out from a pile of bedclothes. In the mornings he no longer woke crying for milk; he pulled himself up, reached for the teddy and sucked the ribbon. When it was completely soaked he began a one-sided conversation, giggling and shouting until Joseph gave up any ideas of staying in bed and went over to the cot to lift him out.

Before Matteo's arrival mornings had been misery for Joseph. Getting out of bed was a daily disaster, struggling to reach for the alarm and turn off the piercing ring. Minutes later it would start again, the shrill sound echoing round the room. But now there was no mechanical wake-up call. The day began with that first smile of the day and the feel of small arms round his neck and the silky head on his shoulder.

When Matteo was in an incubator in the hospital, notes were taken every hour and the slightest change was shared between the nurses and the parents. At home Joseph had no-one to tell when Matteo learned to roll over from his front to his back or months later, to clap his hands. Instead they had an understanding between them: the baby was beginning to recognise language and had a clear grasp of meaning. The word 'no' elicited a widening of the eyes; 'more' was a sound that brought an extra helping of food. Matteo had an invented patter of his own but Joseph could interpret every new spoken sound.

For most of his twenty eight weeks of life there was barely a moment when Matteo's gaze was not returned by a loving smile. But for the week after the revelation about his blood group, there was no-one there to watch him wake up and no-one to kiss him goodnight. Joseph too was alone, with no partner to tell him he was obsessing about things that couldn't be changed. He went over and over events that caused him pain, and in particular, the day he discovered he was not Matteo's father.

Joseph had been paralysed by shock and anger. He kept away from the hospital and didn't even pick up the phone. Yet however unbearable the news, it wasn't enough to cancel out the weeks of devotion and concern that dominated his life. He tried to blot out the thoughts of the little face with the big eyes, but a polaroid photo of Matteo was propped up on his bedside table and it was the first thing he saw when he woke in the mornings.

For the whole week Joseph had been in a state of confusion. He went through the motions of dressing and shaving.

"If I'm not Matteo's father, there's no connection between us."

He ran the razor over his chin and up and down the sides of his cheek.

"And so, if there's no connection, why should I bear the responsibility of bringing him up?"

But there was no 'if'. The information on his donor card was conclusive. The doctors had explained that only a DNA test can prove that you are the father, but a simple blood test can show that you're not. Since there was no other possible father on the scene, Joseph had no choice. He was the only one who could look after Carla's child.

But could he trust himself? He was so angry that he'd tried to make Matteo ill by mixing up the wrong feeds. He'd added extra powder to each bottle, knowing the over-rich mixture might be harmful. If he couldn't deal with feelings of anger against a baby, what would happen when the boy was throwing tantrums at the age of two, sitting on the floor in the supermarket, refusing to move till he was given an ice cream? Or when he was twelve, swearing he had no homework and everyone else in his class was staying up till midnight watching films on TV? By the age of fifteen he'd be growing his hair into an unwashed ponytail, maybe colouring it purple or red.

*

Joseph undressed and lay on the bed listening to the calm breathing in the cot next to him. The worries were beginning to recede. At one time he'd thought Matteo might be deaf, because he didn't turn his head at a sudden noise. Every possible outcome had been imagined—with dreams featuring visits to ear specialists and the fitting of hearing aids. But the fears had proved unfounded, attributed to 'late development', so Joseph tried to block out thoughts of what might have happened, or what could still happen. He turned his mind to practical questions.

They couldn't go on sharing a room for ever; the boy would need his own bedroom with the walls covered in posters of pop stars and footballers. He'd need somewhere to go when they'd had a row, when he was sulking and didn't want to come back to the table to finish his meal. Joseph was wondering if there was any training to teach fathers how to deal with all this? If you could choose from surf science and applied golf management at university there must be a parenting class that would help him avoid confrontation, help him understand why children behave as they do at each stage of their development. But he'd learned one lesson that night: when Matteo pushed the pea up his nose, it had released not just a flow of blood but a torrent of emotion for his father.

CHAPTER 45

'I should have asked him' thought Tom, as he walked away from the concert hall. 'I should have asked what happened to his wife. I just rambled on and talked about the accident and the police.'

As Tom crossed the road he thought how rude he'd been, going on about Sophie's death and not giving a thought to the other man's wife. It had been a strange exchange—when he mentioned the accident the man seemed to go into a state of shock. Why had the news of Sophie's death affected him so badly? But maybe it wasn't that. Perhaps it was post-concert nerves or embarrassment at being accosted in the street.

When Tom arrived home the late news on television was coming to an end. He put the concert programme on the glass table and poured himself a whisky. The conversation on the pavement in Wigmore Street kept coming back to him. "What happened. How did she die? Was she ill?"

Tom had just told the man that his wife had died from an accident. Why should he have been so concerned? From the way he was behaving he must have known Sophie. But that was ridiculous. This man wasn't a friend of Sophie's. He was someone

Tom had met by chance at the hospital. Perhaps he'd been a fellow student at university? But no, an Italian pianist wouldn't have been at Southampton. Tom tried to remember the names of Sophie's friends and went to look for her address book. He ran through the list, mentally ticking off the ones he'd met and others he'd never heard of. There was no mention of Maggiore in the M section. He kept thinking of the expression on the man's face when he'd told him; how his hands seemed to be shaking. Perhaps meeting Tom again reminded him of the hospital and something bad that must have happened to his own wife.

And yet ... maybe there was some connection. But Sophie didn't go to concerts. Museums yes, but concerts? There was one thing; those notes that Tom had found in the hotel room in Lisbon, the slips of paper with the names of concert halls there.

And then it struck him. Wasn't there another note about a hotel? What was it called? It sounded American like Days Inn or Comfort and he remembered that the note said it was near some park. Tom went to the computer and looked up Lisbon hotels. He came up with several possibilities. Was it likely that Sophie was going to meet someone in this hotel and was it possible that the man was Joseph Maggiore? Tom dialled the code for Portugal followed by the first number. A voice answered:

"Eduardo VII Hotel"

"Excuse me, I believe a friend was staying in your hotel last August. Could you check if I've got the right place?"

"Yes sir. What's the name?"

"Joseph Maggiore. I think he was there on August 27th".

"Sorry, no one of that name stayed here."

Tom tried three hotels with the name Comfort. The first two came up with a negative response. He called the last one, the unpronounceable Embaixador. A Portuguese woman replied:

"Cfort Otel, Lijboa".

Tom repeated his request. There was a silence.

"Are you there?"

"Yes, but ees not posble. We can't reveal the names of our guests. If he was here, ees private."

It was strange that the other hotels had been prepared to answer the question and this one was not. It suggested that they'd found Maggiore's name on the register. Tom imagined he was doing a crossword puzzle. He'd got some of the clues across and was now trying to fit in the answers to the down clues. He made a mental note of what he knew: the name Joseph Maggiore; a hotel in Lisbon where he'd possibly stayed at the time of their visit to the Ritz; a note mentioning some concert halls. This was ridiculous. What was he trying to prove? That Sophie and Maggiore were linked in some way? Certainly there were some questions to answer: why had she taken new clothes from London and pretended she'd bought them abroad? And the small gifts, like the expensive belt he'd found in the cupboard, who were they for? More mysterious was the museum catalogue for an exhibition in Bonn. As it happened they never went there, but why would Sophie have gone to the trouble of getting the catalogue in advance, when she could so easily have bought it at the exhibition?

Tom began to look through Sophie's side of the desk. In the drawers were some birthday cards, addressed and ready to send to her niece and nephews. She was organised, always thinking ahead, so was it surprising that she would have bought a museum catalogue in advance? Even if that could be explained there were still two gaping blanks: what was Sophie's connection with Maggiore and why had she kept it secret?

Both of these questions might have been solved but for one moment of recklessness. Tom had thrown away Sophie's mobile phone. He had some memory of chucking it in a bin, but wherever it was, it certainly wasn't at home. At the time he thought it was of no use to him, but if he'd kept it, he could have checked her messages and found out if she'd been seeing Maggiore.

To fill in the missing gaps, Tom did the equivalent of consulting a crossword dictionary. He'd always been able to solve a clue by searching through anagrams or finding an alternative spelling. To explain Sophie's link with the concert pianist, he would have to go over the details of her behaviour, every quarrel, every change of mood or unexplained remark.

He started by concentrating on their trips abroad. Their days ran in parallel, never together. If he had a few hours free between meetings they rarely met. She didn't seem to want him to go to exhibitions with her, saying there was no point as they walked round at a different pace. She liked to spend much longer looking at each painting, analysing the brush strokes and searching for detail, while he had already glanced at all the works on display and was ready to move on into the next room. Then there were the evenings when she never wanted to go out. She used to like going to restaurants, trying unfamiliar food and laughing with him over some of the tastes: the raw herring in Amsterdam, the bacalhau in Lisbon. But there were times when she simply refused to leave the room and persuaded him to order something from the hotel kitchen. It was as if the shopping and the museums had used up all her energy.

The part he found hardest to think about was the sex—or more accurately, the lack of sex. He'd put it out of his mind. Sometimes they'd go for weeks and neither of them would seem interested. And then, one of them would try to recreate the early days of their passion, to bring back the glow that needed so little to spark it into life. Sophie had bought some La Perla underwear and for a while she liked him to watch her undressing. She couldn't wait for him to come to bed, dangling the lace lingerie in front of his face, dropping it at his feet, as he stood there bemused. But then there were times when she looked at him with a detached, almost cold expression and he wondered what was going through her mind. It was then that he was gripped with a fear that he was losing her.

Sometimes he thought Sophie was suffering from a kind of illness. The clothes buying was a mystery and at one time he had explored the possibility of getting her to see a doctor. Yet she could hardly be described as a shopaholic. She was intelligent and selective; she could well afford the items that filled her wardrobe. She had no eating disorder that could be linked to compulsive buying, nor did she have the problems of worry caused by spiralling debts. He'd read about a recovery centre in Kent which treated patients suffering from a range of addictions. According to the doctor there, compulsive shopping was a problem to rank alongside alcoholism and gambling. When Sophie's extravagance reached a crescendo in Bologna and Florence, Tom considered consulting this man, but in the end did nothing. Yet why on earth would she buy dresses in Bond Street and pretend she'd bought them abroad? Unless ... unless she never did buy clothes in Europe and was passing the time doing something else? There was no way of checking to find out how Sophie spent her money. Tom had a large standing order paid into her bank account every month. She preferred to use cash rather than credit cards so there would be no record of what she bought. He had no idea of the cost of a Louis Vuitton handbag, so he'd never know if she had money left over to buy presents for a lover.

CHAPTER 46

The crossword puzzle was still incomplete. It was as if the clues had a theme—a single sentence linking certain words. Tom needed to find the link. He knew so little about Maggiore. He'd had two conversations with him, the one on the pavement and the one in the cafeteria. That was when they'd talked about his piano playing and his favourite composers. He'd said something about his wife. Tom remembered that she was in a coma too, like Sophie, but there was something else; something about her condition. She hadn't been hit on the head. What was it? Yes. She was pregnant. That was it.

Tom began to construct the scenario: Sophie had met Maggiore in Italy, probably at a museum. They'd got talking in front of a nativity scene and he would have been impressed by her knowledge of art. He might have offered to show her round his home town. Over the next few days he'd have taken her to his apartment, furnished with antiques, in a fashionable area. That's where the affair would have started. She'd have begged him to come and see her in London and she'd have shown him the Tate Gallery before taking him back to their bed in Maida Vale.

The pictures in his mind made Tom feel sick, but he couldn't stop them. It was like those books of pictures that turn into animated images with the flick of a finger. Sophie must have arranged a meeting in Lisbon where he'd been playing in some concert. The scribbled note with the name of the hotel was where he was staying. All through the autumn they had carried on seeing each other, usually in Greville Place when Tom was out at meetings. They'd go to the bedroom, move the crimson throw out of the way. They were planning how to spend Christmas together. That was it. Sophie seemed so miserable around that time. That's why she was unwilling to invite her family, to make all the arrangements and order the food.

Maggiore must have broken the news that his wife was pregnant and told Sophie he couldn't see her any more. That would explain Sophie's anxiety. Of course, she was desperate. At the beginning of January she was tormented by jealousy of the wife's pregnancy. But why would Sophie have been jealous? The last thing she wanted was a baby. She'd been adamant about that, telling him repeatedly that babies cried and snivelled all the time and needed changing every hour. He might actually have welcomed the idea of having a child—well, maybe not the small baby kind, but a little boy you could take to football or a girl who would adore her daddy. Why hadn't he simply suggested they should hire a nanny, to get them over the first two or three years? If Sophie had been a mother, it would have solved the dinner party problem. She might have had more friends, joining in the talk about schools and birthday parties. It would almost certainly have made her less obsessed with clothes. She'd once told him what a pleasure it was to wear a blouse with flowing sleeves that wafted down as far as her fingertips, telling him that you could never serve up a dinner to friends in such an outfit.

If Sophie never wanted to be pregnant why would she have been so distraught by the news of Maggiore's wife's condition? A simple explanation occurred to Tom: She was planning to go away with the pianist; but he was constrained by his impending responsibilities. He was the cause of all her misery. So on that fateful day she had walked out into the road in Maida Vale and thrown herself in front of a car.

The whisky bottle was almost empty. Tom felt his eyes closing and leaned back in the chair. He woke up with a start and glanced at the clock. It was the middle of the night; he'd been hunched up, dozing, for hours. His neck ached and his mouth was dry. He dragged himself on to the bed, pulled a sheet over his clothes and fell asleep.

*

The next morning he made himself coffee and opened a new jar of black cherry jam. The butter oozed over the toast and a spoonful of the fruit softened into the warmth, nestling inside the darkened edges of the crust. While he was eating the first mouthful, he put another two slices of thick granary bread into the toaster. After breakfast he didn't bother to move the unwashed mug and plate to the sink. For once he didn't take the trouble to scoop up the crumbs and wipe over the granite top. He went into the bathroom and shaved.

The thoughts of the previous night came back to him and he dismissed them as the miserable musing of a drink-induced haze. The idea that Sophie was having an affair with Maggiore was nonsense. If it was true, she would have tried to conceal it. But she didn't seem particularly secretive—on the contrary, she was relaxed. There was an explanation for everything: the notes about concert halls meant nothing. She'd probably wanted to go out one evening and found that there were no theatre performances in August. The slip of paper with the hotel name—well, maybe she'd found somewhere that might have been of interest to him, for his work. Even if Joseph Maggiore had stayed there, it didn't prove anything.

In trying to understand Maggiore's extraordinary reaction and the odd clues in Sophie's behaviour, Tom wavered between two possible explanations. He'd almost convinced himself that his suspicions were entirely unfounded. After all, they were perfectly happy as they were, living a comfortable life in London and travelling together to luxury hotels in European cities. And then the nagging doubts came back.

Sophie could not bear the thought of someone else having Maggiore's child.

Was it possible that Sophie might have committed suicide? What was it the policeman had said? 'Would you say your wife was happy?' 'Maybe the driver was faced with something beyond his control.'

She had certainly not been herself in the last few weeks, though he hadn't told any one, of course. It wasn't the sort of thing you'd mention. Not to her father, or her sisters. All the time he'd been blaming himself; trying to find a reason for her despondency. Now it was all coming clear. She was having an affair with Maggiore. He wanted to end it. She wanted to die.

CHAPTER 47

Was there any point in confronting the man? What would he say? He'd be sure to deny it. He'd hardly admit to something that couldn't be proved. And the clues? Bits of paper with notes; a collection of museum catalogues; clothing bought in London and taken abroad. Was there the slightest proof that these had anything to do with Maggiore? No, it was better to leave it.

But then, if Tom were to arrange a meeting, he could come straight out with it; accuse the man of having an affair with his wife. He'd be able to see from his reaction if he was lying. But then again, unlike that first encounter outside the concert hall where he'd been taken by surprise, Maggiore would know what was coming. He'd have time to prepare an explanation.

It didn't make sense to dwell on something that might never have happened. Tom decided to put the whole matter out of his mind and picked up a folder of correspondence. He had two new artists lined up. One was a woman called Candida who was turning out hand-painted seascapes at the rate of twenty a week. The other, a recent graduate of St. Martin's College of Art, had impressed the judges at his degree show with the way he combined rope, sand

and pebbles. Either of these would be perfect for neutral colour schemes in sunny rooms. 'Maybe Maggiore was with Sophie in a sunny room, in Bologna, in Lisbon?' Suspicion is like a squirrel nibbling away at a nut, storing the uneaten half under a bulb in a flower pot, ready to dig it out in the winter when there's nothing to be found on the ground. Tom kept mulling over the doubts that had been sown in his mind since the confrontation that he himself had initiated.

In an attempt to concentrate on his work, Tom looked for brown paper and bubble wrap so he could make a package of the sand and stone collage. He'd already wrapped four of the unframed seascapes. He threw a change of clothes into a bag, rang for a taxi and put his mind to choosing a destination. Since the first time when he'd chosen Madrid at random, he'd got into the habit of rushing off to the airport with little idea of where he was going. He was too distracted to make arrangements in advance and with no commitments back in London, it hardly mattered how many days he was away. In June he'd chosen to fly to Munich and Rome; happy to find an empty seat next to him and relieved that there were no children squabbling in the row in front—it was too early for family holidays.

With his bag packed he sat and waited, closing his eyes to conjure up a map of Europe. He ran an imaginary finger along the coastline of the south of France and Italy, wondering which resort would be a suitable showcase for his marine paintings.

Tom stood up and went to the front door. He was so used to standing there, with his keys in his hand, calling out to Sophie 'are you ready?', that he still found himself stopping for a moment before he went out.

'I could find out when his next concert is and corner him afterwards. He wouldn't have time to prepare a response' he thought.

Tom was confused, not knowing whether to keep picking away at the scab, or to leave it. The taxi was pulling up. He needed to be decisive, to stop wavering. A destination came into his mind: 'I'll go to Naples.'

Italy was where he felt comfortable, yet he couldn't bring himself to go back to a city where he'd been with Sophie. It was too painful to return to Florence or Bologna alone, not for the memories of the hotels where they'd stayed or the restaurant where they'd sat at a corner table, but for the more unsettling moments. He'd be walking in a street and suddenly come across a building, in a colonnade perhaps, where he'd recall an argument about why she'd kept him waiting when all she had to do was go shopping. People think it's the happy memories that bring on the tears, but for him it was the concentration of bad thoughts; the small irritations, the arguments, the unfinished discussions, all the times when he wished he'd said something different.

CHAPTER 48

On that day when Sophie had walked out in front of the car, they'd had a row over breakfast. Tom was clattering the plates and putting them in the dishwasher. Sophie was silent, nursing her mug of tea while he bustled around her, eager to get back to work after the long Christmas break. It had been more than usually tense, with a visit to Gemma on Christmas day and a series of drinks parties culminating in a dismal event on New Year's Eve. A hundred guests were crammed into a loft in Islington with pulsating dance music and a slide show of the hosts' holiday in Cambodia flashing up on a screen. At midnight there was the usual orgy of kissing with people who hardly knew each other shouting 'Happy New Year'. The first two days of January had been uneventful with Sophie curled up in the Barcelona chair and Tom planning his next trip abroad. It was the mention of Portugal that sparked off the row. Tom had said something about how miserable she'd been the time they went to Lisbon and he hoped she'd cheer up when they went to Bonn. She had launched into a tirade about taking your problems with you when you travel and he'd lost his temper, yelling at her that she was his only problem and that he'd go without her next time.

The thought of that icy day came back to him as he climbed into the taxi. The memory of the quarrel made him shiver but as the cab wound through the back streets on the way to the M4 he felt himself sweating in the summer heat. He opened the window and put his hand inside his jacket, feeling under the arm of his shirt to see if it was as wet as he imagined. What was he doing, going to Naples in August? The hoteliers would be too busy to see him and he'd brought the wrong clothes for a hot and dusty city. Perhaps he should change his mind and go further north? By the time he arrived at the airport he began to feel agitated. He tried to make a mental agenda of the meetings he would set up, but he was in no state of mind to appreciate the obvious advantage of travelling alone. With no one to consult he could make instant decisions, but all he could think of was the prospect of walking into a restaurant on his own. The Maitre d' would show him to a table with a good view of couples dining together. There'd be an interminable wait for the food and a waiter hovering, pouring wine as soon as he'd taken a sip. Each dish would be eaten in a matter of minutes. All the time he'd be wondering where to look, not to be seen staring. Reading was not an option—it would imply so clearly that this was a necessary meal, rather than a night out with company and conversation.

Tom found an internet connection and wondered if he should force himself to go back to a familiar city, instead of making things difficult for himself by choosing Naples. He typed 'Florence' into the search engine and started to scroll down the list of events near the city. Not far away was a town called Arezzo. It seemed to have a square like Siena, with a similar steeply sloping brick pavement. There was also a church with frescoes by Piero della Francesca. 'Sophie would have liked that' he thought. He put his hand over his eyes, squeezed the temples and let out a long breath. He ran his fingers over the mouse again. He came up with an event called the Giostra del Saraceno. It looked interesting; something about teams competing in a jousting competition, but he'd missed it; it was in

June. He closed the window on the computer and went back to flight options.

He planned to be away for two days. With Sophie the usual pattern had been four days, long enough to arrange some meetings and be back in London for the end of the week. The short breaks were the springboard for the follow-up discussions with the artists. He couldn't wait to get back, eager to conclude the deals and find out how much profit he was going to make from selling the work to the hotels. But since her death the excitement had gone. There was no incentive to make more money. Tom was beginning to regret this trip. He was already imagining sitting in some cafe, trying to make a cappuccino last half an hour, staring at groups of youngsters, laughing, talking. He still hadn't bought a ticket. He looked up at the board and saw that there was a flight leaving for Milan in an hour. A thought came into his head: he'd forget about work and do something completely different. He was tired of setting up meetings, being polite to people who were having difficulty speaking English. Instead he'd go and please himself.

He had a scheme in mind. With the ticket in his hand Tom stood on the concourse, surrounded by travellers. There was a family with two children, wearing pink and blue backpacks, poking each other—tired already, even before their flight. A woman in a sharp trouser suit and pointed high heels was tapping at her phone. He wondered how they were seeing him: a businessman in his early thirties on his way to conclude an important deal? For a moment Tom considered tearing up the ticket and going home. He was moving towards the departure lounge, carried along in a line of passengers preparing themselves for the next hurdle, the security check: jackets off, keys in the bin, men with artificial hips smiling an explanation as they activated the metal detector. Tom picked up his overnight bag and placed it on the conveyor with the two packages. Behind him in the queue was a woman wearing a long printed skirt. She was twisting her hair into a coil and pinning it up with a crystal-blue hair comb. It matched her eyes. Tom wondered for a moment whether she was wearing tinted contact lenses.

As he went to collect his belongings, one of the paintings began to slip out of his grasp. The woman reached out a hand and rescued it before it hit the ground.

"Wow, that's heavy. What have you got in there? A paving stone?"

"No, no. it's just a painting."

"It's not 'just a painting' if you're the artist, so I guess you're not."

"No, I'm not. But I work with artists. It's complicated."

Tom waited for her to respond. He was reluctant to move away, so they found themselves walking through to the seating area, looking for an overhead screen to check their gate numbers. By coincidence, both of them were searching for the same destination. By this time Tom had discovered that her name was Astrid Johanssen and that she worked for a company importing Danish crafts.

"So how does that take you to Milan?" he asked, trying not to stare at the piercing blue eyes.

"There's an exhibition there called Finger handvaerk—that just means crafts." she said.

By now they were at the gate, waiting to board the plane. Tom wanted to continue the conversation. Astrid seemed so uncomplicated. She was straightforward and softly spoken. Everything about her was tranquil. He couldn't remember the last time he'd chatted up a woman. It was as if he'd forgotten how to play the game. While he was thinking of something clever to say in response, she solved the problem for him by pushing a card into his hand.

"Pop in and see me when you get back to London. I can show you what I've bought."

Tom slid the card into his jacket pocket and gathered his baggage together. He would have liked to ask about her dealings with artists, to compare notes. Instead he smiled and mumbled:

"Astrid Johanssen ... I'm glad we met."

Two hours later he walked to the passport control at Malpensa airport. On previous visits to Milan he'd often hesitated in reply to the question 'Business or pleasure?' believing that the two were linked, but now he was planning a few days of sheer indulgence. He would have no need of the pictures and was wishing he hadn't brought them with him. Once he had checked into his hotel—a 1930s palace—he was relieved of his burden. He closed the door and carefully lowered the paintings on to the floor. He reverted to his old habit of talking out loud to himself:

'I don't believe in luck. Destiny is another matter. Perhaps that meeting at the airport was meant to be?'

Years in the hotel business had taught him that Milan was the style capital of Italy and he knew exactly where to go. He made straight for the furniture showrooms on Corso Monforte and Via Durini. The first task was to find a replacement for the Barcelona chair. He'd get rid of the buttoned leather beast that had caused so much friction; the chair that Sophie rarely sat on because it was so uncomfortable.

Sophie wasn't the only one who could spend his money. Tom found himself reaching for his credit card as he bought seating from Armani Casa and wall panels of shaded light. As he read the description—'pragmatic elegance for hard times'—he was reminded of his conversations with Sophie about the pretensions of the dress designers. He chose a scarlet bed called 'Breakfast', armchairs with head rest and 'loin rest' and stools with a spindly steel frame covered in ponyskin. The last purchase was a purple chair designed to hang from a ceiling. He could imagine it already—once he had moved to another flat, filled with the new furniture, far away from Maida Vale. He could see the purple chair in the living-room. There would be steps leading down to a coffee table set in a pool with electric blue fish swimming among the stones. The walls in the bedroom would be denim and the floors stripped pine. There'd be no hard surfaces in the kitchen; no gravestone granite, but a warm veneer on the cupboards and solid wooden worktops. Like a photograph in a pool of developing liquid, slowly becoming clear, the picture in his mind was taking shape: he'd get rid of all the old stuff and start again with everything new. This time there'd be no discussions with dealers; he'd take it all round to the local charity shop—everything, except for the frying pan. He'd need the old one for the fry-up.

Tom closed his eyes and a faint smile came to his lips as he dreamed of floating a large lump of butter into the pan, sizzling in the bread till it was crisp. Maybe three eggs would be a bit too much, but he'd certainly need a large tin of creamy baked beans and an extra slab of butter to fry the banana.

Sophie had gone along with all his foibles, rarely criticising his pernickety ideas on style. Retreating into their flat after an evening out, they'd laughed at their friends' pretensions and reassured each other that they were happy—just the two of them—with no children. Of course there had been the odd argument but there was no simmering discontent. After five years of marriage the attraction that had brought them together was still there, with no sign of it diminishing with time.

Sophie might have been depressed. But suicide? Nothing in her manner revealed a truly disturbed state of mind. Maybe he'd been too preoccupied with his work and missed the signs? What good would it do him to torment himself over his lack of attention before her death? And then, how would it help him to go over and over the way it had happened? In a split second her life had ended.

He had a choice: he could either accept what the police were implying, that it was simply 'an accident', or he could spend his life searching for someone to blame. That could be the driver, himself or Maggiore. If he chose the first option—that it was an accident—he could remember Sophie as she was—beautiful, happy, laughing. Their years together had brought him joy and intimacy; the moments of dissent far outweighed by an overriding sense of togetherness. They had shared two disparate lives in an amicable way, learning to appreciate the other's enthusiasm, but arguing playfully about day to day nonsenses and obsessions.

Or he could take the alternative path, continuing the search for a truth which might never become evident: he would spend his life in anger and frustration, unable to solve the puzzle, yet never able to put it out of his mind.

His journey to Milan had already presented him with a third option: as well as building a new home with the furniture he'd bought, he could also begin to envisage a new life. A question crossed his mind: 'are tinted contact lenses changed every day or once a month?'

CHAPTER 49

For several nights after the nosebleed Joseph was unable to sleep, tossing and turning in the August heat. It was only in the silent hours that he could face the news of Sophie's death. The encounter with Tom had left him in a state of shock made worse by the impossibility of showing his grief. As soon as he'd returned home, he'd had to leave immediately for the hospital and the worry about Matteo's loss of blood had pushed everything else out of his mind. Maybe he'd got it wrong; that it was another Sophie who had died; a different Tom who'd told him about it. But it all made sense. Why else would she have failed to return his calls? Why wouldn't she have contacted him? His thoughts began to weave between Carla lying in a coma and Sophie fading away after the car had hit her. Sophie died first. It was a week or so later when Carla slipped away. Where were they now? If there was a heaven, would they meet? Would they realise he'd loved them both and failed them both? Would they compare notes on what he was like as a husband, a lover? Would they complain about his piano playing, his selfishness? In one part of his imagination there was a heaven that was filled with soft clouds and the music of Mozart and Bach.

In another was a limbo where souls were waiting. Reserved for him would be the inferno of Dante, the words he'd learned in school coming back to him: 'nel mezzo del cammin di nostra vita'. He'd certainly lost his way in the middle of life's journey. And the 'dark woods' referred to in the first canto of the poem? He was surely there.

Joseph woke from his dream to hear Matteo gurgling happily. He leapt out of bed and ran to collect the post, hoping to find the score of a new piano concerto. Before he could open his letters, the doorbell rang and there was Richard, grinning.

"So, how did it go?"

"What? Oh, the concert at Wigmore Hall. That was fine but we had a bit of a drama when I got home."

After he'd told Richard about Matteo's visit to the hospital, Joseph went back to the subject of work:

"You know this new Arensky concerto I'm going to play? I've only heard it once but it's dramatic, just like Tchaikovsky."

"It's a bit of a departure for you, isn't it?"

"Well, it's certainly different from the Mozart sonatas. I'm not sure my hands are right for it. The other thing that makes me nervous is Arensky's fascination with irregular time signatures."

"Is that a problem?"

"You wouldn't understand." Joseph started to rip open the envelopes.

"You're so superior. Why wouldn't I understand? I'm the one who gets you the work, remember?"

"You have no idea, do you Richard? You just breeze along, thinking everything will be all right. You don't know what goes into these performances. You just think anyone can get up on the stage and play like Uchida or Brendel. You don't realise the hours and hours of practising ... and I've got Matteo not well, and I'm doing it all on my own, without any help."

"Hang on, Joseph. Where's all this coming from?"

"It's coming from up here, in my head. I don't know, I just can't concentrate."

"Come to think of it, Arensky probably had difficulty playing it himself" said Richard after a few moments.

"What do you mean?"

"Well, after all, he was a gambler and an alcoholic. He was the worse for wear most of the time."

"What have clothes got to do with it?"

"Sometimes I think you pretend not to understand."

"I understand you very well. It's like you to find out the chiacchiera, the how you say, gossip? You never say anything good about people, do you?"

"Only the ones I'm promoting."

Joseph glared at him and continued to open his post. Richard wondered if he'd forgotten the breakfast invitation. There was no sign of any croissants or French bread on the table. He turned and walked back to the door:

"You're obviously in a foul mood, so I think I'll go."

"No don't do that. Go and make yourself some coffee while I deal with Matteo."

The noise from the bedroom had changed from gurgling to an insistent wail.

"O dio. He needs breakfast. I forgot we don't have any cereal. I bet Arensky didn't have to pop out for a box of cornflakes when he was working on his 5/4 tempo."

Richard went into the kitchen, opened a cupboard and took out two mugs. He reached up for the Moka express, put water in the base and pressed the ground coffee into the top compartment. As he was opening the drawer to get spoons he noticed Joseph standing in the doorway.

"I see you know where things are."

"Well, yes. I ... I've seen you do it."

"But this thing doesn't work. It leaks. I haven't used it for months."

"So how do you make coffee now?"

"I just do it in a jug and then I strain it."

Matteo was crawling round the floor. Richard picked him up and held him in the air.

"He's not going to be sick, is he?"

"Not if you stop wiggling him around. Anyway, he's almost stopped. It's been much better since he's been on the soya milk."

Joseph held out his arms and made a funny face. Matteo started to giggle.

"When do they start to talk?" asked Richard.

"When they've got something to say, I expect."

Matteo was holding out his hand and saying 'bab, bab'.

Joseph passed him a piece of bread.

"See, he doesn't need to talk. I know what he needs."

Richard realised that Joseph was in no mood to talk either. In an attempt to improve the atmosphere he said:

"You're good with him, aren't you?"

"Hmmm?"

Joseph wasn't listening. He was pouring a cup of soya milk and brushing crumbs off Matteo's T-shirt.

"You seem to do it all so naturally."

At that moment Matteo knocked over the cup and a pool of milk spread across the table. Joseph grabbed the letters and began to wipe them with a cloth. Matteo was dipping his fingers in the milk and wiping them on his hair.

"I'm going to give him a bath."

"I thought you only gave children baths in the evening."

"Eh, that would make sense if they only got dirty after supper." said Joseph.

He began to run in the water. Richard was standing by the bathroom door.

"He's lucky. You're a pretty good Dad."

Joseph took off the nappy and lowered Matteo into the water.

"Hey. How's that? Nice and cool?" he handed the baby a pile of bath toys and while Matteo was moving little pots from one hand to the other, Joseph squeezed a sponge over his hair.

"A good Dad? I suppose I'm the best he's got."

*

Joseph seemed happy sitting on the floor with water splashing over the side of the bath. Richard was still holding the door handle. He found it hard to imagine dealing with a baby. He supposed he'd have to unbutton his cuffs and roll up his sleeves. For a few ghastly days, after he'd heard that Carla was pregnant, it crossed his mind that he could have been the father. But she never said a word to him, so it obviously hadn't occurred to her. How could it, when theirs had been a five-minute fling and Joseph was sleeping with her all the time? Thank God Carla had never referred to that dreadful afternoon. She'd obviously made up her quarrel with Joseph and put it out of her mind.

With no prospect of coffee or breakfast it seemed a good time for him to leave. Joseph was on the phone asking the babysitter to take Matteo out for a walk so he could practise. Richard was about to call out some jokey comment when he stopped. He'd never thought about it before; the total responsibility, the lack of freedom, the liability of looking after a child. You couldn't read the paper in the morning, couldn't go for a drink in the evening, and in between there was hardly a moment when you could concentrate on anything that didn't involve the baby. How the hell did Joseph manage to play the piano at all?

CHAPTER 50

Joseph had dressed Matteo in clean clothes and sat him down at the table with some grapes and the remains of a stale bread roll. When he turned round Matteo was beaming a wide smile. He was sucking one of the letters, holding out an envelope. The paper was torn and the corner was completely wet.

Joseph grabbed the letters and began to straighten out the envelopes. At that moment Annabel arrived:

"Sorry I'm late, Mr. Maggiore. I had this friend texting me and he was like ..."

"Don't worry" said Joseph, distracted. "I suppose I'm lucky you can come at all during the day. How much longer do you have before you go back to school?"

"A couple more weeks. Do you mind if my friend comes with us? He's good with babies. His mum's got six."

Joseph couldn't imagine dealing with a large family. He looked at the damp letters and thought what damage another five children could have done in those few minutes. He put aside the bills and took out the sheet music he'd been waiting for. It came with a short biography of Anton Arensky. It didn't say anything about the drinking and gambling but it mentioned that he started composing at the age of nine and wrote the F minor concerto when he was twenty one.

Annabel was strapping the baby into the buggy and promised to be back in a couple of hours. She'd already arranged to meet her friend in the park, so she didn't wait for a response. It hadn't crossed her mind that Matteo's Dad would mind if she wasn't giving the child her undivided attention.

Joseph went into the kitchen and picked up the broken coffee machine. He was about to put it back in the cupboard when he remembered another occasion when he'd been in the kitchen with Richard. They'd had some conversation about the glasses and how Carla couldn't reach them.

'How did Richard know where everything was? How was he so familiar with the coffee maker, the mugs?'

He must have been here several times before. Perhaps he'd been here with Carla. Alone. That was the solution to the puzzle. The man was Richard.

"Sono pazzo. I must be mad" shouted Joseph, out loud.

"Of course it was him. He would have known when I was out. He knew where I was playing; how long it would take me to get home."

He had a vision of Richard taking off the jacket of his new suit, drinking coffee in the kitchen and then following Carla into the bedroom and watching as she slipped off her clothes. Joseph slumped into a chair.

"Oh Sophie, what do I do?"

The heat in the flat was intense. Joseph opened the window and looked out. There was no-one there to hear him speak:

"So, he made love with Carla. If I ask him, what will he say? Do I tell him he could be Matteo's papa? What if he decides he wants Matteo, if he takes him from me?"

It would be disastrous to raise the matter. Joseph was imagining Richard taking a DNA test to prove his paternity and arriving on the doorstep with an empty suitcase, ready to be filled with baby clothes and toys. He'd be walking out of the door and Joseph would be left standing in a silent flat. On the floor by the cot, would be Fred, left behind in the confusion, the ribbon still wet from the last time it had been passed through Matteo's lips. But there had never been the slightest indication that Richard was interested in the baby. If he'd wanted to claim his rights as a father, he'd have done it by now. He wouldn't have waited for seven months. On the other hand, maybe he would; maybe he'd wait till the boy was walking and talking. Why else would he ask when a child starts to speak? At school Joseph had found it hard to invent stories, to come up with imaginative essays in class. Now he was thinking up possibilities at the rate of an airport novelist working on a deadline for the following month. He ran through one fantasy after another, each one with a confused structure and what his teachers would have called 'muddled thinking.' Joseph's rambling led him further away from any solution. This was a problem with no obvious conclusion. The uncertainty in his mind grew more insistent.

"So, it may be someone else? Carla had the chance to invite anyone to her bed. How will I ever find out? Which is better: that it is Richard who I know, or another man I don't know?"

There was another question: what to tell Matteo? He imagined the boy coming home from his first day at school with a letter addressed to his parents. He'd open the envelope slowly and he could explain again how his mother had died. But he couldn't follow that with the comment 'and I'm not sure who your father is, either.' When should he consider telling him the truth? Five was too young to understand the facts of life, let alone the details of sordid infidelities. He could tell Matteo that babies come from a seed that grows in a special place inside the Mummy. Then he could say that the Daddy helps when his seed combines with Mummy's to make the baby start to grow. He couldn't begin to tell him that it wasn't actually Daddy, not this Daddy, but another man who had got his seed inside, damn him. Was it right to keep the truth from Matteo? That whoever his father was, it certainly wasn't Joseph. He could wait till the boy was fifteen, when he'd understand about men and women and desire. Wasn't that when his own education had started? Or maybe eighteen, just as he was about to start university? There was an alternative: he could make up a story that he and Carla had adopted him. There would be no question about who had brought him up and loved him from the moment he was born. That would certainly be better than turning his world upside down and leaving him with an insoluble problem: how to find the man who had been his mother's lover. But isn't there a law that says an adopted child is entitled to know who his real parents are? Trying to switch off these miserable thoughts Joseph went back to the piano to start work on the Arensky concerto. He remembered the excitement of starting a new piece, his fingers moving over the skeleton of the harmonies, fleshing it out with tone and tempo. Being alone was part of the pleasure, having no interruptions. But now instead of an exquisite isolation Joseph was overcome with a feeling of desolate solitude.

He had always wanted to be a soloist, never part of a trio. He'd only ever wanted a wife. A marriage was for two. He had broken the bond the moment he'd taken Sophie to the cafe in the park. For an instant he thought of Tom. He too never chose to be part of a threesome. Together, with Richard, they had become enmeshed in a sextet of sadness. And the sixth player, Matteo? He had emerged unharmed from his perilous birth. Joseph knew it was up to him to give his son the life he deserved.

*

Outside there was a screeching of brakes; a car driven at speed was turning round, reversing, moving forward again in a three point turn. A child was skipping along the road. At the station a man disappeared into the underground. On the platform a dozen passengers waited for a train. Mobile phones went quiet.

Far away in a distant place a hand reached out but in the soft whiteness there was no reception, no communication, silence.

THE END

The idea for Sextet came to me some time ago on a long haul flight. I wrote the plot and finished a first draft in a couple of months. Then the manuscript sat in a drawer for years while I published a children's cookbook and devoted my energy to writing *The Armchair Kitchen*, my daily blog on food.

Those who helped me in the early days might be thinking I had forgotten them. Now the novel is out I want to thank them for their valuable contributions.

I am grateful to David Court for allowing me to spend a day with the team at St. John's Wood Ambulance station in London. Dr Rodney Rivers updated me on current developments in neonatal care at St. Mary's Hospital.

In the real-life situation that formed the basis of Matteo's story we received exceptional care from the late Dr. Harold Gamsu and the staff at Fred Still Neonatal Ward, King's College Hospital. I am also indebted to the charity BLISS for their warm and encouraging support to parents of premature babies. My friend C.J. Jackson (no relation) shared with me her personal experience of pancreatitis.

Paul Sears checked and improved my Italian. Tim Jackson commented on an early draft of the manuscript. Emily Marbach cast a literary eye on the later version. Barbara Arden-White gave me useful advice. Daniel Halfon was generous in the time he spent working on audio ideas. Rachel Jackson took time off her studies in Chicago to design the text. The cover illustration is by Rebecca Jackson, not yet in college and already a talented artist.

Above all I want to thank my husband Michael. How many authors have an editor and computer consultant who is ready to drop anything at the slightest request? Apart from being a man of infinite patience, Michael is a reader who takes pleasure in words. He is an authority on the works of George Eliot and Anthony Trollope. My inability to write like them must be a source of disappointment to him, but he disguised this in his willingness to discuss every minute detail of the book. Now the work on Sextet has come to a close, I imagine he is glad to get back to his role as chief taster in food related projects.